Unyŏng-jŏn

KOREA RESEARCH MONOGRAPH 33

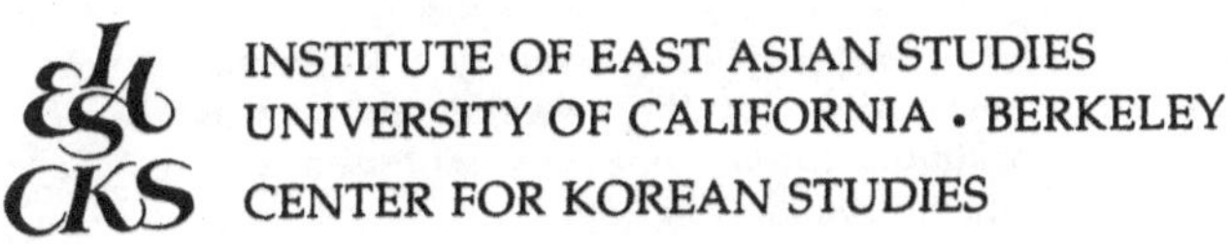
INSTITUTE OF EAST ASIAN STUDIES
UNIVERSITY OF CALIFORNIA • BERKELEY
CENTER FOR KOREAN STUDIES

Unyŏng-jŏn
A Love Affair at the Royal Palace of Chosŏn Korea

INTRODUCTION AND ANNOTATIONS
Michael J. Pettid
TRANSLATED BY
Kil Cha and Michael J. Pettid

A publication of the Institute of East Asian Studies, University of California, Berkeley. Although the institute is responsible for the selection and acceptance of manuscripts in this series, responsibility for the opinions expressed and for the accuracy of statements rests with their authors.

The Korea Research Monograph series is one of several publications series sponsored by the Institute of East Asian Studies in conjunction with its constituent units. The others include the China Research Monograph series, the Japan Research Monograph series, and the Research Papers and Policy Studies series.

Send correspondence and manuscripts to
Ms. Kate Chouta, Senior Editor
Institute of East Asian Studies
2223 Fulton St., 6th Fl.
Berkeley, California 94720-2318

Library of Congress Cataloging-in-Publication Data

Pettid, Michael J.
Unyong-jon : a love affair at the royal palace of Choson Korea / introduction and annotations Michael J. Pettid ; translation Kil Cha and Michael J. Pettid.
p. cm. -- (Korea research monograph ; 33)
Includes bibliographical references and index.
ISBN 1-55729-093-8 (alk. paper)
1. 880-01 Unyong chon. 2. Love stories, Korean. 3. Korean fiction--17th century--History and criticism. 4. Women--Korea--Social conditions--17th century. I. Pettid, Kil Cha. II. 880-02 Unyong chon. English. III. Title.
PL989.A1U5936 2009
895.73'2--dc22

2008039464

Cover image: Library of Congress, LC-USZ62-72640

Contents

Acknowledgments

This project began during my postdoctoral studies at the University of California at Berkeley, where I was fortunate enough to have "rediscovered" *Unyŏng-jŏn* in the Asami collection while working on another project, a serendipitous discovery that was to eventually redirect my entire project. The staff and faculty at the Center for Korean Studies at Berkeley, particularly Clare Yu and Jonathan Petty, were extremely helpful in all matters during my stay and assisted this project greatly. The postdoctoral fellowship itself was funded by the Korea Foundation. The Korean Literature Translation Institute provided a generous grant for the translation project, and that grant helped provide the time and resources for this volume. Haechang Choung of the Academy of Korean Studies kindly provided the copy of the Changsŏ-gak version of *Unyŏng-jŏn* that I also used in this translation.

My translation in this volume benefited from the expert assistance of many during the lengthy process. Colleagues here at Binghamton such as Zu-yan Chen in Chinese literature were of great help in solving problematic parts of the translation. JaHyun Kim Haboush of Columbia University provided helpful comments for the improvement of the manuscript as did the anonymous reviewers for the press. In all, the end work benefited greatly from the comments of many colleagues, both here in the States and in Korea. Finally, my thanks to the Institute of East Asian Studies at Berkeley and Managing Editor Joanne Sandstrom for guiding the manuscript through the publication process.

Any errors, omissions, or oversights are, of course, my own. I have endeavored to create an accurate translation, and I believe that the translation of *Unyŏng-jŏn* presented here meets that criterion and will stand the test of time. As with any translation, decisions had to be made in regard to the best word or phrase for items in the original text that do not have close matches in English. I hope that the choices I made have resulted in an enjoyable translation of a work first conceived some three centuries ago in a set of social circumstances quite different from our own. It is also my hope that this work will allow scholars and students access to a true jewel of not only Korean premodern literature, but premodern literature in general.

CHAPTER ONE

Introduction

In Chosŏn Korea of 1601, a socially inept scholar, Yu Yŏng, decides to experience the wondrous beauty of the Inwang Mountains, and alone ascends the mountain and enjoys a bottle of wine he had carried with him. He happens upon a beautiful woman and young man sitting together and joins their company, asking them who they are and why they have come to this mountain. After much prodding, the two reluctantly agree to tell their story. The woman, named Unyŏng, begins her story by telling Yu that she was once the palace woman of Prince Anp'yŏng (1418–1453) and that the young man with her was a *chinsa* by the name of Kim.[1] Anp'yŏng was a great lover of literature and the arts, and when dissatisfied with the literary level of the men of the day, decided to train ten of his palace women, one of whom was Unyŏng, in letters. Anp'yŏng always guarded the women closely, never revealing their presence to any outsiders. Yet one day, Unyŏng met Kim and a forbidden love affair exploded.

Thus unfolds the story of Unyŏng and Kim *chinsa*. This early-seventeenth-century novel follows the winding path of the secret love affair between these two and the difficulties they encounter in attempting to realize their desires. The novel holds all the elements needed for a truly captivating story: love, treachery, heartbreak, danger, and friendship.

Unyŏng-jŏn [The tale of Unyŏng] is noteworthy among premodern Korean novels in several respects. First, it is generally said to be one of the very few premodern romance novels with a tragic conclusion. Most commonly, Korean novels featuring a love affair end happily as seen in works such as *Ch'unhyang-jŏn* [The tale of Ch'unhyang]. Even heroic novels featuring a love affair such as

[1] The literary licentiate (*chinsa*) was the first major stepping-stone toward passing the government service examination (*kwagŏ*).

Cho Ung-jŏn [The tale of Cho Ung] have gratifying conclusions. Perhaps because readers desired happiness in their own lives, novels—works created largely for entertainment—carried such endings.

Also notable in *Unyŏng-jŏn* is the narrative structure. The narrative voice is largely that of Unyŏng, and the story unfolds through her eyes and experiences. *Unyŏng-jŏn* is the first Korean novel to utilize a female narrator. Thus, this novel evolves through Unyŏng's space, emotions, and experiences. Consequently, it offers readers an opportunity to enter a very restricted space in the Chosŏn dynasty (1392-1910), the world of the palace women who served at the royal palaces.

Given the woman's voice and view prominent in this work, *Unyŏng-jŏn* demonstrates how women grappled with the difficulties brought about by the very restrictive Confucian ideology of the seventeenth century. Through the voice of Unyŏng and her fellow palace women, we gain insight into the hardships these women experienced in matters such as the realization of love and the loneliness of isolation. The reader also will understand the comradeship between the palace women, who all suffered under the restrictive rules governing their lives at the palace. In such aspects, *Unyŏng-jŏn* is one of the very few premodern Korean records of any sort depicting a woman's understanding of life.

Finally, *Unyŏng-jŏn* is notable for its focus on the issue of human freedoms. The central theme of the novel is that of basic rights of humankind: the right to select a lover, the right to follow one's own choices in life, and the right of women to have rights equal to those of men. The author of this work had a clear vision for a more equitable society, and this work was the forum for introducing basic human autonomy. Debates and conversations in the text present vivid arguments for the realization of basic rights to readers. For an early-seventeenth-century work, *Unyŏng-jŏn* is centuries ahead of its time in the quest for basic rights that are taken for granted at present. Such a historic call for autonomy is unrivaled in the fiction of this period in Chosŏn.

While the genre of the novel was held in contempt by many upper-class elite males in Chosŏn, it nonetheless was greatly popular among women. Accordingly, we should understand *Unyŏng-jŏn* as being reflective of the desire of many women for the realization of love and personal fulfillment. The fact that this work was widely circulated demonstrates that it matched a need among readers during the last half of the Chosŏn dynasty.

Unyŏng-jŏn taps into the tremendously deep and rich tradition of literary Chinese in East Asia. More than a work of Chosŏn Korea, this novel draws from the then two-thousand-year-old literary legacy of China in creating a very complex narrative interspersed with cues and markers for the reader. Such signposts would have signaled the educated reader of the seventeenth century as to impending conflicts or served to heighten interest. Readers of the day would have easily caught clues conveyed through the use of metaphoric words or phrases, allusions to ancient legends or personages, and references to poets or poetic styles. Yet this very same complexity and depth creates a formidable barrier for the reader of the twenty-first century.

For this reason, the present work is more than simply a translation of a seventeenth-century novel written in literary Chinese. Cognizant of the complexities in premodern literary works, in this work I seek to create a bridge between the reader of today and a literary creation of some three centuries ago. Accordingly, I begin with a close inspection of the social conditions that prevailed in the early to mid-Chosŏn period, the very atmosphere reflected in this novel. An essential element for understanding this novel is an understanding of the restrictions placed on women in Chosŏn.

Following the introduction of the social backdrop for *Unyŏng-jŏn,* this work examines the institution of palace women in Chosŏn. Because the fictional Unyŏng and her comrades depicted in *Unyŏng-jŏn* were palace women, it is necessary to understand their lives. At any given time in the Chosŏn dynasty the number of women in servitude at the royal palaces was about six hundred,[2] not an insignificant number. Beyond simply numbers, palace women are also important in that they were educated women who were able to record their songs and narratives. Similar to the women portrayed in *Unyŏng-jŏn,* some palace women had deep knowledge of the literary traditions of East Asia and were able to record these in writing.

An examination of palace women will further allow the reader to understand how and under what restrictions these women lived. The elites of Chosŏn had a propensity to codify nearly every aspect of life, and this immense legal framework closely governed the lives of palace women. Consequently, we can see the procedures in which a woman would be selected for service at the royal palace and the training that she would subsequently

[2] Kim Yongsuk, *Chosŏnjo kungjung p'ungsok yŏn'gu,* 25–27.

undergo. Also, the heavy restrictions that marked their lives are also prominent and permit recognition of the mental duress these women suffered. The position of palace women in Chosŏn was a unique one in that they were not often granted natural "freedoms" that were allowed, indeed required, for almost all other women, especially in terms of fulfilling a woman's role in childbearing.

Important considerations with *Unyŏng-jŏn* and any other premodern text are matters of the creation, propagation, and distribution of the work. While this task is not an easy matter with any text of this age, this investigation is made all the more onerous by the way in which the genre of the novel was viewed by elite Chosŏn society. Poetry was held as the highest literary form in all of East Asia, and perhaps to an even greater degree in Chosŏn than in neighboring countries. Fictional works such as the novel were heavily criticized to the level that writers oftentimes left their works unsigned to avoid official censure. This is well illustrated by the case of the high official Ch'ae Su (1449–1515), who was dismissed from his post for writing a novel and then translating it into hangul.[3]

Accordingly, the fact that *Unyŏng-jŏn* is unsigned is not surprising, especially given that the novel was coupled with a content that subverts principles basic to the foundations of Chosŏn society. Whoever the writer might have been, we can surmise that he or she was well-educated and familiar with life at the royal palace. Such an individual would not risk censure by signing a controversial work.

Because of the obvious literary skill manifested in the text, the authorship of *Unyŏng-jŏn* is most commonly attributed to a man of a high status. Yet a reading of the work reveals a narrative told from a woman's viewpoint, something unlike any other mid-Chosŏn-period fiction. The reader sees society very much through a woman's eyes and emotions, to such a degree that one must ask if a woman could have written this work. That question is a primary concern of this book.

The distribution of *Unyŏng-jŏn* is also a murky trail. Coupled with the low status of the novel form in Chosŏn was an official disdain for commercial activities. So while the commercial market for books thrived in both contemporary China and Japan, it was

[3] *Chungjong sillok,* 14:25a (1512-09-02), 14:27b–28a (1512-09-18), and 14:29a–29b (1512-09-20).

weak in Chosŏn; this is true for literature in general and even more for a disdained form such as the novel. Thus the conditions for commercial printing and distribution of books did not exist in Korea as elsewhere in East Asia.

Yet despite official scorn, novels in general were very popular among women of upper-status groups and some commoners. Notwithstanding the prevailing conditions of the country not being good for the commercial publication of books until the nineteenth century, there was demand for copies of novels. This led to the transcription of books for circulation along with book-lending shops that catered to this ever-expanding market. As a result, novels such as *Unyŏng-jŏn* were widely circulated and read.

Presently, there are more than twenty versions of *Unyŏng-jŏn,* both in literary Chinese and in hangul. There are also versions that were rendered into Japanese in the early twentieth century.[4] While the plot and essential story line are similar in these works, the fact that there are numerous versions of the novel testifies to its continuing popularity in Chosŏn and beyond: different editions demonstrate that readers were actively engaging with the novel for at least three centuries after its creation.

Unyŏng-jŏn is an excellent character study of divergent personalities ranging from a rival for the throne to a lowly slave. It is, perhaps, this quality of complexity that sets this novel apart from other works of the period. Rather than flat, one-dimensional characters, *Unyŏng-jŏn* is laden with realistic characters that open a new window to understanding life in the Chosŏn dynasty. The fullness of the characters in the novel is best seen in Unyŏng, who steps off the three-hundred-year-old pages of this work and into the presence of the reader.

---

[4] See Cho Hŭiung, *Kojŏn sosŏl ibon mongnok,* 453–455.

CHAPTER TWO

Historical Backdrop

The dynastic change from Koryŏ (918–1392) to Chosŏn (1392–1910) marked the rise of Confucian ideology as a governing system and way of life in Korea. While this ideology had been present in Koryŏ, it was not given supreme status within the government and played a secondary role to Buddhism in the customs of the people.[1] This was all the more true in the lives of women, who enjoyed substantial rights in regard to economic and social matters in Koryŏ. Chosŏn was to be a period in which women were to lose a tremendous amount of freedom as their lives became heavily influenced by the Confucian vision of womanly virtue and an ever-strengthening patriarchal system.

Chosŏn Dynasty and Change

Yi Sŏnggye (1335–1408), the founder of the Chosŏn dynasty, was able to usurp the Koryŏ dynasty through a combination of military power and support from those later designated as meritorious elites (*kaeguk kongsin*). While it is sometimes argued that the so-called newly risen literati class (*sadaebu*) came into prominence at this time, in fact there was a great deal of continuity from Koryŏ to Chosŏn in terms of the Confucian scholar group; some Koryŏ Confucianists even opposed the new dynasty out of loyalty.[2] While the aims of the meritorious elites and the literati class often clashed in the first two centuries of Chosŏn, both advocated changes to the existing social systems. In particular, the two groups composed a scholar-official class that spearheaded various changes designed to create a society that reinforced their positions of privilege.

[1] Confucianism entered the Korean peninsula in the fourth century via China.

[2] John Duncan, *The Origins of the Chosŏn Dynasty*, 237–238.

The scholar-official class was heavily influenced by the reformed Confucian philosophy first explicated by the Cheng brothers (Cheng Hao [1032–1085] and Cheng I [1033–1107]) and Zhu Xi (1130–1200) of the Chinese Song dynasty (960–1279).[3] The teachings of this school sought to overcome the philologically oriented Confucianism then in vogue, advocating instead a political ethic found in ancient Chinese literature that elucidated the mutual relationship between ruler and subject.[4] By adding a metaphysical aspect to Confucianism, these men created a Confucianism that was much more all-encompassing and was able to become a worldview that demanded compliance to all of its tenets throughout society. The supporters of this ideology saw the ruin of Koryŏ as the result of misgovernance brought about by the Buddhist foundations of the state. Thus, to men such as Chŏng Tojŏn (1342–1398) reformed Confucianism represented not only a means to construct an orderly society but also a way to create a bridge with the prominent Confucian history of Korea, dating to the age when Kija was given the fiefdom of Chosŏn by King Wu of the Zhou dynasty (1027–771 BCE).[5]

It was in this atmosphere that the elites of Chosŏn set out to reform society and create a system that supported their positions of privilege. Among the early targets of the reformers were belief systems such as Buddhism and shamanism. Buddhism was seen as corrupt and antisocial, and Buddhist mass gatherings, with the volatile mingling of men and women, were condemned as being ruinous to the country. Not surprisingly, the countrywide Buddhist festival, the P'algwan-hoe (Festival of the Eight Vows), was banned early on in Chosŏn.[6] Shamanism and its rituals were also

---

3 For an overview of Yi Sŏnggye's rise to power and the role of literati class see the above cited work by John Duncan; Ki-baik Lee, *A New History of Korea*, 162–178; or Carter J. Eckert et al., *Korea Old and New, A History*, 100–124. For an excellent discussion of the changes that the literati brought about after the foundation of Chosŏn see Martina Deuchler, *The Confucian Transformation of Korea: A Study of Society and Ideology*, 89–129. For an examination of the impact of the new ideology on the lives of women, see Ch'oe Sukkyŏng and Ha Hyŏngang, *Han'guk yŏsŏng sa: Kodae Chosŏn sidae*, 313–326; or Kim Yongsuk, *Han'guk yŏsok sa*, 85–126.

4 Haechang Choung and Han Hyong-jo, *Confucian Philosophy in Korea*, 2.

5 Deuchler, *The Confucian Transformation of Korea*, 107–108.

6 A particularly damning description of the P'algwan-hoe and the evil influence of Buddhism is found in an account in the *Chungjong sillok* 20:26a–26b (1514-04-29). This record faults King T'aejo (r. 918–943), the founder of the Koryŏ dynasty, for not purging the popular customs at the onset of the dynasty. The entry continues to condemn Buddhism for its "lewd music and beautiful women who could easily bewitch those men near to them."

disparaged by Confucianists as being immoral rites (*ŭmsa*), and various laws were aimed at eradicating shamanic practices.[7] In fact, the persecution of either worldview would have been tantamount to attacking both, since by the twelfth century the two systems had intermingled to the point that they were virtually inseparable.[8]

The persecution of Buddhism directly touched the lives of women not only in the practice of this worldview, but also in restricting gatherings with other women. It has been argued that the primary concern of early administrators in regard to women was in keeping them at home, and the biggest worry was the visits of women to temples.[9] Because legislators wanted to establish Confucian ideals for proper womanly behavior (*pudŏk*), women were to be kept away from the corrupt influences of Buddhism, particularly the mingling of the sexes that was common at temples. Thus, the dynastic record of the first years of Chosŏn is dotted with complaints against Buddhism, accounts of women who violated the laws in visiting temples, and calls for further restrictions.[10] Significantly, early legislation in Chosŏn prohibited women from upper-status-group families (*yangban*, the two orders of officialdom) from visiting Buddhist temples and gathering for ceremonies or festivities where there might be mixing of the sexes. The punishment for such a violation was one hundred strokes with a cudgel.[11]

Likewise, *yangban* women were also prohibited from visiting shamans or attending shamanic rites. These were viewed as

During the reign of King T'aejo (1392–1398) a proposal to prohibit the P'algwanhoe was entertained. *T'aejo sillok* 1:51a (1392-08-05). Yet the decree evidently did not end the festival altogether, as can be seen by the fact that there were subsequent bans on the festival.

[7] By the reign of Sŏngjong (1469–1494) various laws were in place to restrict shamanic practices such as a prohibition against shamanic practitioners plying their trade in the capital and members of the upper *yangban* class participating in shamanic rituals. The enforcement, however, was lax and consequently a call was made to enforce these measures more diligently. See *Sŏngjong sillok* 10:44b (1470-06-18); 88:20a (1477-01-20).

[8] Yu Tongsik, *Han'guk mugyo ŭi yŏksa wa kujo*, 168.

[9] Ch'oe and Ha, *Han'guk yŏsŏng sa*, 304.

[10] For example, see the *Sejong sillok*, 30:10b (1425-11-08) and 30:14a (1425-11-15. for an account condemning the wife of an official who frequented a temple with other women of the upper class.

[11] The *Kyŏngguk taejŏn*, 4:7a, prohibits women of scholar families from visiting temples and forbids *yangban* women from attending night rituals (*yaje*) or celebrations.

corrupt, and moreover, as at Buddhist temples, such rites provided an occasion for the mixing of the sexes. Indeed, a central point of similarity between Buddhism and shamanism was the fact that both allowed men and women to be together in an uncontrolled environment—or at least an environment not controlled by Confucian dictates. Royal edicts degraded the social standing of shamans along with Buddhist clergy, pushing them and their belief systems further from mainstream society.[12] Moreover, shamans soon were barred from even living within the walls of Hanyang (present-day Seoul), and women of upper-class families were prohibited from attending shamanic rites.[13]

Not only was the *yangban* woman guilty of such misconduct subject to punishment according the Chosŏn legal code, so too were her descendants. The repercussions for the family and descendants of a woman who behaved in an inappropriate manner were significant, including ineligibility to sit for the civil service examinations. For example, the sons of a woman deemed guilty of misbehavior or who remarried were not allowed to serve in either the civil or military bureaucracy.[14] Moreover, the sons and grandsons of such a woman were not allowed even to sit for a variety of civil service examinations.[15] Although the raft of legislation contains some inconsistencies, the main points are clear enough: a woman's actions could easily thwart the careers of her male descendants. Given the wide range of offenses that could be penalized, families sought to protect their future prosperity by closely guarding the actions of their womenfolk.

The overall thrust of Chosŏn society aimed at keeping upper-status-group women at home, thereby limiting the possibility of contact with men outside their families and elements that the Confucian lawmakers deemed inappropriate of a woman of high status. One petition to the throne in 1449 declared,

> Women [of the upper status groups] have no business outside of the home. In the provinces, upper-class wives, sometimes under the pretext of serving as a pallbearer, sometimes that of attending a religious rite, go out with all sorts of liquor and meats. They

---

12 For example, the descendants of shamans, Buddhist clergy, *kisaeng* (female entertainers), and others were barred from receiving stipend lands. See *T'aejo sillok,* 4:14a–14b (1394-12-28).

13 For example, see *Sejong sillok,* 53:3b (1431-07-13), 53:5a–5b (1431-07-17), 101:34b–35a (1443-08-25).

14 *Kyŏngguk taejŏn,* 1:4b–5a.

15 Ibid., 3:1b.

> gather openly and impudently make merriment to their hearts' content. This is a dirty custom.[16]

The petitioner adds that such shameless and brazen mingling of men and women had caused Chinese envoys to laugh and declare that the womanly ways of Chosŏn had gone seriously awry. The elites of Chosŏn wanted to cleanse society of such behavior and accordingly created the body of regulations, social norms, and penalties collectively known as the *nae-oe pŏp* (rules of the inner and outer). The inner refers to women while outer indicates men; we can understand this set of regulations as being aimed at keeping the sexes apart (except in specific situations) and strengthening patriarchal society.

In essence, the *nae-oe pŏp* sought to restrict women to their homes and isolate them from men other than their close relations. Women would not be able to leave their homes at their leisure or have contact with men aside from relatives, and the women who did would be guilty of misconduct and of not practicing fidelity.[17] The enforcement of such a strict system of controls was part of the overall push by the ruling elites to create a strong patriarchal and ordered society.

While laws and social practices were strongly directed at recreating Chosŏn as a Confucian society, we must remain aware that such a transformation was an ongoing project and one that was never fully realized. Buddhism and shamanic practices never disappeared, even among womenfolk of the uppermost status groups. These worldviews provided important relief for the people and could not simply be purged because of the desires of the ruling elites. This is all the more true for women, who needed such nonregulated spaces for mental release from the strict regulations of official Confucian society.

Education and Social Change

Key to creating such a Confucian society was education. The link between literature and Confucianism was prominent to the elites of the early Chosŏn period. Although they had different ways of understanding literature, for both the meritorious elite, now referred to as the Hungup'a (Faction of the meritorious and conservative), and the Confucian moralists (the Sarimp'a, the

---

[16] *Sejong sillok,* 123:4a–5a (1449-01-22).

[17] Yi Sun'gu "Chosŏn sidae ŭi sŏngnihak kwa yŏsŏng," 185–186.

faction of the *sarim*) the relationship between literature and cultivating the Confucian way was understood as indivisible.[18] Such a worldview dominates the discourse on education in early Chosŏn.

The dynastic records of the early years of Chosŏn are replete with requests and plans regarding the education of the people. The need for such education was keenly felt by the ruling elite, who often attributed the fall of the previous dynasty to the moral degradation of the people.[19] Along with these calls for educating the people, other records recount the immoral behavior of those who corrupted the people in past times. The *Koryŏsa* [The history of the Koryŏ dynasty], compiled in 1451 by a team of scholars headed by Chŏng Inji (1396–1478), contains numerous accounts of the immoral behavior of Koryŏ kings and other personages.[20] The other major record of the Koryŏ period, *Koryŏsa chŏryo* [Essentials of Koryŏ history] compiled by Kim Chongsŏ (1390–1453) and others in 1452, has similar accounts of misbehavior of the Koryŏ court, at least in the eyes of the Chosŏn Confucianists.[21] The oftentimes biased accounts in these records can be said to reflect the desire of the literati who composed it to justify Yi Sŏnggye's usurpation.[22]

The introduction and enforcement of Confucian ethics in Chosŏn resulted in fundamental changes to the existing society and the worldview of the people. While this affected all people, it can be posited that Confucianism affected the lives of women in a significantly more negative way than it did men. Yi Sun'gu cites the creation of binary relations of hierarchy in the Confucianism after the Warring States period (403–221 BCE) in China as the root of the problem.[23] While there was always a distinction between

---

18 Pak Hyŏnsuk, *Chosŏn kŏn'gukki ŭi munhak-ron*, 12–13.

19 For example, see *T'aejo sillok*, 8:8a–9b (1396-10-05).

20 Similar accounts of royal debauchery can be found concerning King Ch'ungnyŏl (r. 1274–1308), *Koryŏsa*, 31:12b; and King Kongmin (r. 1351–1374), *Koryŏsa*, 43:22a–22b among others.

21 Although the accounts in this work are not as descriptive as those in the *Koryŏsa*, we can still find references to misbehavior concerning the royal family such as a 1343 entry concerning an adulterous relation during the reign of King Ch'unghye. See *Koryŏsa chŏryo*, 25:24b–25a.

22 Edward J. Shultz notes of this, "Chosŏn scholars, anxious to substantiate the legitimacy of their dynasty, presented Koryŏ history in a highly critical light." See *Generals and Scholars: Military Rule in Medieval Korea*, viii. Thus, despite the fact that the *Koryŏsa* was based on records from Koryŏ, it reflected the beliefs of the Confucian literati of the early Chosŏn period who edited and amended the work.

23 Yi Sun'gu "Chosŏn sidae ŭi sŏngnihak kwa yŏsŏng," 163–165.

yang and yin, the relationship was initially without hierarchy. After the Warring States period, however, Confucianists began to categorize all things according to a hierarchy of yang (heaven, noble, positive, light, male) and yin (earth, mean, negative, dark, female), contingent on the superiority of yang qualities. Yi thereby contends that women came to hold an elementarily inferior position to men in the Confucian world.

Confucianism from its beginnings oftentimes viewed women in a negative or, at the very least, subservient light. In the early Classics of Confucianism we can find representations of proper behaviors for women that would carry major repercussions regarding women for some two millennia. For example, the *Lizhi* [Book of rites] established exemplary ethics for women in terms of womanly virtue (*pudŏk*), fidelity (*chŏngjŏl*), and the three obediences (*samjong chido*).[24] While the interpretation of these ideals would change over the centuries, the presence of strong patriarchal-type features in early Confucianism demonstrates a major aspect of this worldview, namely, the subordination of women to men.

The procreative power of women has also been cited as a reason for the rise of gynophobia early in Chinese history. Sandra A. Wawrytko writes that "even a good (Confucian) woman could be a threat to men, despite her best intentions, simply through her biologically and cosmically grounded womanliness."[25] With such a backdrop, Confucian texts came to suggest that women necessarily should be controlled for the good of society, and this view was reinforced by the desires of the elites to create an orderly society in Chosŏn.

There were other reasons behind the oppressive conditions for women in Chosŏn. The *Lizhi* states that the performance of ancestral rites is the most filial act a son can perform for his parents and is an extension of his service to them while they were alive.[26] In the Koryŏ dynasty, however, women were able to officiate over ancestral rights and as a consequence could inherit economic resources that enabled the performance of these rites. This practice was to change in Chosŏn. Martina Deuchler argues that

[24] Chŏng Chaesu, "*Yŏllyŏ-jŏn* ŭi yŏsŏng yuhyŏnghak," 17. The three obediences are that a woman should first follow her father's opinions, and then her husband's after marriage, and finally those of her son after the death of her husband.

[25] Sandra A. Wawrytko, "Prudence and Prurience: Historical Roots of the Confucian Conundrum Concerning Women, Sexuality, and Power," 176.

[26] *Lizhi*, 545–546.

male-led Confucian ancestral rites that reduced or eliminated the official role of women in the rites brought fundamental change to Chosŏn society. Since only a son could perform ancestral rites and as a consequence inherited resources from the family, the spread of these rites solidified the fundamentally superior position of men over women. An outgrowth of the better male position was a lowering of a woman's economic independence over the first half of Chosŏn, and this made her increasingly dependent on her husband.[27]

Aside from the metaphysics of Confucianism and the enforcement of ancestor worship, we can cite the simple desire of men to control the sexuality of women as an additional reason for the strict regulations of Chosŏn. The rules of the *nae-oe pŏp* created the perfect social control for the sexuality of women. If a woman was confined to her home and allowed contact only with close male relatives, the chances of illicit sexual relations were substantially less than if she was allowed freedom to move about. Feminist discourse argues that patriarchal systems emerge from the desire of men to protect their "right" to father children with a woman. To achieve this end, various rules, penalties, and inducements are enacted throughout society, providing men with the tools to regulate the bodies of women.[28] In this respect, the Confucian society of Chosŏn was no different from any other patriarchal society in regard to the treatment of women. As such, we can expect to find patterns both of legislation and of education designed to reinforce and strengthen patriarchal aspects of society while at the same time weakening the position of women.

An area that was quickly a target for lawmakers was that of remarriage for women. Restrictions on the remarriage of upper-class women had been enacted by late in the Koryŏ period. Yet, for various reasons, such restrictions were not always enforced. For example, Yi Sun'gu mentions the economic problems involved with the support of women who were widowed at a young age. With the help of legislation devised in early Chosŏn, by the late fifteenth century the idea of remarriage as being something impure and undesirable for women was solidified.[29] The creators of the *Kyŏngguk taejŏn* laid out penalties for the descendants of a

---

27 Deuchler, *The Confucian Transformation of Korea*, 135.

28 A detailed discussion concerning forms, implementation, and socialization can be found in Kate Millet, *Sexual Politics*, 24–58.

29 "Chosŏn sidae ŭi sŏngnihak kwa yŏsŏng," 171.

woman who had remarried, thus revealing the direction in which society was being steered.[30] The purity of women was essential to maintaining the purity of the *yangban* bloodlines, and consequently remarriage was anathema to the lawmakers. This was, perhaps, the cruelest aspect of Confucian ethics as it forced young widows to live long lives in solitude. Remarriage would cause the ruin not only of their natal family, but also the family that they had married into, by denying the opportunity to serve in officialdom.[31] Marriages, first and foremost, were made between families, and the fact that they would continue after the death of the husband demonstrates the permanency of the marriage bond, at least for a woman.

Hand in hand with the propagation of ancestral rites, prohibitions on remarriage, and the strengthening of the patriarchal system was the ascendancy of the eldest son as the unquestioned head of the family. The maintenance of a patrilineal lineage succession in the household required that the heretofore variable living arrangements be shifted to a strict patriarchal system. In fact, Yi Sun'gu contends that in order to establish Confucianism as the dominant social ideology, the ruling powers of Chosŏn had to change all aspects of society to support and encourage the creation and maintenance of a strong patriarchal family system.[32] The Chosŏn educational system reflects this desire in various ways, especially through the education of women.

It was through the implementation and enforcement of these Confucian ethics that Chosŏn society was remade, thus marking a sharp break with those societies that had previously existed on the peninsula. Of course, the transformation of the age-old customs and worldview of the people would require concerted and ongoing efforts by the ruling elite. Moreover, one should be cognizant that alternative worldviews such as Buddhism and shamanism never disappeared and continued to play important roles in the lives of the people. Nonetheless, by the late fifteenth century there were numerous legal codes in place to encourage correct Confucian behavior. An essential means to stimulate such behavior were the didactic works aimed at fashioning a society reflective of Confucian ethics, and such works were printed and distributed by the government. One of the earliest educational

---

[30] *Kyŏngguk taejŏn*, 1:4b–5a, 3:1b.

[31] Kim Yongsuk, *Han'guk yŏsok sa*, 190–191.

[32] "Chosŏn sidae ŭi sŏngnihak kwa yŏsŏng," 165.

works with this intent was *Samgang haengsil-to* [Conduct of the three bonds with illustrations, 1432], which provided illustrated examples of the three bonds (*samgang*)—loyalty of ministers to the king, filial behavior by children, and distinction of duty between men and women.

Along with formal education were informal methods that helped create a strong patriarchal system. From their earliest days, female children were taught, by both direct and indirect methods, to understand their subordinate status.[33] Social education in Chosŏn society ensured that women were fully cognizant of their inferior position at an early age.

The effectiveness of the informal social education system in shaping the status and self-valuation of woman can be understood by examining some common sayings describing women, their behaviors, and their roles in life. Common utterances concerning a woman's status include *namjon yŏbi* (men are exalted, women lowly), which demonstrates in no uncertain terms the inferior position of women. Other sayings such as *punaech'ŏn* (man is heaven) elevate the status of men, while others emphasize a woman's need to be obedient to her spouse (*yŏp'il chongbu;* literally, a woman must follow her husband). Yet other sayings admonished women to conform to social rules through which they could further the family's interest; this sort of admonition is explicit in the saying, If a woman's voice is heard beyond the middle gate, that family will be ruined (*yŏja ŭi ŭmsŏngi chungmun pakkŭl nagamyŏn kŭ chibi manghada*). Such discriminatory, oppressive, and demeaning sayings helped provide a binary discourse for correct and incorrect womanly behavior in the Chosŏn period. There was little ambiguity in such sayings, and we can posit that such sayings served to sustain notions of inferiority among women themselves.

The influence of the early didactic works and government policies was gradual and took centuries to filter down from the upper layers of society to the lower classes. Moreover, it would be incorrect to state that the values advocated by the elites ever spread to the desired point of saturation. Nonetheless, the value of educational works in governing the country seems clear, and there was a concerted effort among the ruling classes to continue the propagation of Confucian ideals through printed media. A 1512 entry in the dynastic record demonstrates both the dismay

---

33 Kim Youngsook Harvey, *Six Korean Women: The Socialization of Shamans*, 263.

that some had with the state of customs and the hope for altering behavior with enlightening works:

> Nowadays the *samgang* [three bonds] have crashed to the ground. Customs are disorderly, the people have lost their original character, and kindness and gentleness are unknown. In the time of the late king, in order to strengthen the *samgang* and *oryun* [five relationships], a book recording the portraits and achievements of loyal retainers, filial sons, and virtuous women was made. The book, *Samgang haengsil*, was distributed to the capital and provinces and moved the common people. How could such a work not help with ruling [the country]?[34]

This focus on education as a means of controlling and shaping society would not waver in the sixteenth and seventeenth centuries, and a flow of edifying works sought to make Confucian notions pervasive throughout society.

By the sixteenth century, a male-centered discourse concerning the bodies of women had emerged, and it continued to have significant effect until the early twentieth century. The systematic strengthening of Confucian ideals for women centering on womanly virtue became widespread in the upper classes, and ideals such as not remarrying were held as beautiful virtues.[35] Along with such notions, the concept of maintaining fidelity grew ever stronger and became reified both through educational works designed for women and in narratives glorifying exemplars of such activity.[36] Such efforts to edify the women of Chosŏn in proper Confucian behavior reached a peak after the Japanese invasions of the late sixteenth century and the Manchu invasions of the early seventeenth century.

It was in such a social environment that *Unyŏng-jŏn* was written. While the novel is set in the mid-fifteenth century, the narrative reflects the changes brought about by Confucian notions concerning women up until the early seventeenth century. The restriction of the spaces allowed to women had become much more rigid by this time, and this social isolation is reflected in *Unyŏng-jŏn*.

---

[34] *Chungjong sillok*, 17:4a (1512-10-08). The five relationships are those between ruler and subject, father and son, husband and wife, elder and junior, and friend and friend.

[35] Ch'oe and Ha, *Han'guk yŏsŏng sa*, 305.

[36] For example, the *Samgang haengsil-to* was expanded and reprinted in 1514 as *Sok samgang haengsil-to* [Expanded conduct of the three bonds with illustrations].

Along with a restriction on those spaces allowed to women of the upper classes, the post-invasions period brought about an increasing emphasis on concepts of womanly fidelity and chaste behavior. Perhaps more than all the other restrictions evident on the women of *Unyŏng-jŏn,* the codes concerning fidelity and chastity dangle ominously over the female characters.

Palace Women

Who were the palace women featured so prominently in *Unyŏng-jŏn*? There are records of palace women for all Korean kingdoms dating back to the Three Kingdoms period (1st cent. BCE–7th cent. CE).[37] For Chosŏn, we can note the creation of an administrative apparatus for palace women in 1405, but this seems to have been only the formalization of a system already in place.[38] Palace women held one of seven ranks ranging from the senior fourth rank (*sunsŏng*) to the junior ninth rank (*sasik*). The administrative system for palace women was formalized with the promulgation of the *Kyŏngguk taejŏn* [National code] in the late fifteenth century.

Palace women were part of a larger grouping of women who, in a narrow sense, held official ranks (*naemyŏngbu*) at the royal palace. The greatest number of these women had been invested with an official rank by virtue of marriage to a member of the royal family or a civil or military official.[39] The highest ranks (from senior first to junior fourth), known as *pusil* (small room) were reserved for the wives; below them (holding ranks from senior fifth to junior ninth) were the palace women. The specific ranks were established in the *Kyŏngguk taejŏn* as detailed in table 1. The titles of these positions reflect the duties of the women such as *chŏnsŏn* (cook) and *chŏnŭi* (seamstress). Furthermore, some women assisted the court musicians (*akkong*) by playing simple music during court functions.[40]

Palace women of higher ranks served the royal family directly. And those women who achieved the highest rank are thought to have wielded a certain degree of political power, at least in regard

---

37 See Kim Yongsuk, *Chosŏnjo kungjung p'ungsok yŏn'gu* 4–7; and Sin Myŏngho, *Kunggwŏl ŭi kkot: kungnyŏ,* 18–19.

38 *T'aejong sillok* [Veritable records of King T'aejong], 9:2b (1405-01-15).

39 Ch'oe and Ha, *Han'guk yŏsŏng sa,* 504.

40 Kim Yongsuk, *Chosŏnjo kungjung p'ungsok yŏn'gu,* 9.

Table 1: Women's ranks

Pusil

Grade	Senior 1	Junior 1	Senior 2	Junior 2	Senior 3	Junior 3	Senior 4	Junior 4
Title	*pin*	*kwiin*	*soŭi*	*sugŭi*	*soyong*	*sugyong*	*sowŏn*	*sugwŏn*

Ranks of Palace Women

Grade	Senior 5	Junior 5	Senior 6	Junior 6	Senior 7	Junior 7	Senior 8	Junior 8	Senior 9	Junior 9
Title	*sanggung* *sangŭi*	*sangbok* *sangsik*	*sangch'im* *sanggong*	*sangjŏng* *sanggi*	*chŏnbin* *chŏnŭi* *chŏnsŏn*	*chŏnsŏl* *chŏnje* *chŏnŏn*	*chŏnch'an* *chŏnsik* *chŏnyak*	*chŏndŭng* *chŏnch'ae* *chŏnjŏng*	*chugung* *chusang* *chugak*	*chubyŏnch'i* *chuch'i* *chuu* *chubyŏn'gung*

to directing other palace women.[41] History is also dotted with those palace women who captured the affections of a royal and were taken as secondary wives, thus elevating their status to that of queen or royal consort.[42] Yet we should note that for the handful of women who reached a lofty rank or joined the royal family, hundreds of others at any given time were relegated to lives of solitude.

In a more general sense of the term, "palace woman" can apply to all of the women who worked in the royal palaces to assist the royal family in daily life. This also includes women who did not have official rank, but still lived at the palace and performed some task required by the royal family. Many of the women without rank were those charged with carrying water to the various rooms of the palace or keeping fires burning.[43] There are a few different appellations for these women including *naein* (inside people, i.e., women) and *sinyŏ* (serving women) in addition to the more general term *kungnyŏ* (palace women).

Although the process for selecting palace women varied in Chosŏn, initially the ideal was to select young girls from commoner families (*yangga*). Many families, however, sought to avoid having their daughters conscripted. As a passage from the eighteenth-century diary of Lady Hong reveals, seeing one's daughter selected for service in the royal palace was seen not as ideal, but rather as something to complain about. Lady Hong had selected two palace women—the daughters of men in the employee of the royal palace—but by that very afternoon King Yŏngjo scolded her for her choices. Lady Hong posits, "What must have happened was that Kim Suwan, a close crony of Sŏngguk, did not want his daughter to enter service at the palace, and so he asked Sŏngguk to intervene on his behalf."[44] Such a response by the father demonstrates that even for those within the palace, having one's daughter become a palace woman was seen in a highly negative light.

Why was there such resistance to having one's daughter selected to serve at the palace? Notable perhaps is that the families of daughters selected for service at the royal palace remained

---

41 Ch'oe and Ha, *Han'guk yŏsŏng sa*, 505–506.

42 Kim Yongsuk, *Chosŏnjo kungjung p'ungsok yŏn'gu*, 30.

43 Ch'oe and Ha, *Han'guk yŏsŏng sa*, 505.

44 Quoted in JaHyun Kim Haboush, *The Memoirs of Lady Hyegyong: The Autobiographical Writings of a Crown Princess of Eighteenth-Century Korea*, 280–281.

responsible for their daughters and were required to provide goods and clothing for the coming-of-age ceremony that took place sometime around the girl's twentieth birthday.[45] Too, if a palace woman became seriously ill, she would be sent back to her natal home; the women were not allowed to be gravely ill or die at the royal palace. Given such a burden, families did not wish to see their daughters selected as palace women. Therefore, many palace women were of lowborn mothers such as *kisaeng* (female entertainers) who had become concubines of government officials or female slaves belonging to government offices.[46]

The office charged with procuring young women to serve at the royal palaces was the Naesusa (Palace supply office), which managed nearly all aspects of life at the palace ranging from obtaining everything from food to slaves. After receiving an order, this office would seek out young girls of commoner families. Because many commoner families were loath to see their daughters taken away, they quickly arranged marriages as a strategy to avoid such servitude. The unwillingness of commoner families to see their daughters appointed to the royal palace is seen in an edict issued by King Hyojong (r. 1649–1659) stating that all palace women were henceforth to be selected from the various government offices rather than from commoner families.[47] By the reign of Yŏngjo (1724–1776) this practice became codified in the *Sok taejŏn* [Supplement to the national code] when the selection of commoner-class women as palace women became prohibited.[48]

Life as a palace woman could start quite early for some. While the norm seems to have been selecting girls aged about ten, some were selected and taken to the royal palace at ages as young as four.[49] Upon entering the palace, each girl was assigned to a senior palace woman who acted as her mentor and taught her rudimentary duties.[50] Along with their work, the girls were also instructed in hangul and elementary Confucian works such as *Xiaoxue* [Elementary learning] and *Nusishu* [The four books for women]. It is notable that palace women comprised one of the very few groups of women who received a formal education in

45 Kim Yongsuk, *Chosŏnjo kungjung p'ungsok yŏn'gu*, 36.

46 Ch'oe and Ha, *Han'guk yŏsŏng sa*, 510–511.

47 *Hyojong sillok* [Veritable records of King Hyojong], 11:43a (1653-09-24).

48 *Sok taejŏn* [Supplement to the national code], 5:20b.

49 Ch'oe and Ha, *Han'guk yŏsŏng sa*, 511.

50 Kim Yongsuk, *Chosŏnjo kungjung p'ungsok yŏn'gu*, 37.

letters in Chosŏn. Along with such indoctrination into proper behavior, the women would also be trained in essential matters needed for palace life including how to sit and bow properly, how to walk softly, how to speak properly (i.e., using the correct manner of honorific speech used at the palace), and how to write.[51]

These well-educated palace women created a substantial body of literature. Lengthy prose works such as *Kyech'uk ilgi* [Diary of the year *kyech'uk* (1613)] and *Inhyŏn wanghu-jŏn* [The tale of Queen Inhyŏn] are attributed to palace women; additionally, there are scores of poems and shorter works such as the *kasa* poem-song "Kungnyŏ-ga" [Song of the palace women]. Such a body of works authored by palace women is certain to grow larger as research extends deeper into the huge body of unsigned premodern works.

Notwithstanding the above examples, most palace women did not have the opportunity to perfect their literary skills. Most served their masters in the royal palace through more menial pursuits and received only the basic education required to instill proper behavior for life at the royal palace.

The number of palace women serving in the various palaces is difficult to ascertain, and is thought to have fluctuated with time. Kim Yongsuk cites numerous historical documents in placing the number of palace women at about 600 at any one time.[52] We can thus see that the number of palace women was significant and represents a sizable percentage of those in servitude at the royal palace. An interesting comparison to the number of palace women is that the number of eunuchs (*hwan'gwan*) serving at the palace at any one time approached only 240.[53]

Palace women, based on their rank, were also provided a monthly stipend, making them a relatively rare example of an employed woman in the Chosŏn period. The salary would have been paid in the form of cloth necessary for clothing and also the rice and other foods needed for daily life.[54] While their salaries were not on the same scale as those paid to men and not always fixed, the fact that they were paid is an interesting one. Records further indicate that in times of crisis or drought, the stipends

---

51 Ibid.

52 Kim Yongsuk, *Chosŏnjo kungjung p'ungsok yŏn'gu*, 25–27.

53 *Han'guk minjok munhwa taebaekkwa sajŏn*, 25:408.

54 Sin Myŏngho, *Kunggwŏl ŭi kkot: kungnyŏ*, 194–195.

given to palace women were reduced.[55] The stipends thus varied depending upon the country's finances.

The actual working circumstances for palace women seem to have mainly depended primarily upon the number of palace women employed by the government at any given time. An entry in the dynastic record from 1414 states that the hardships suffered by the palace women were not due to the drought plaguing the country, but rather the fact that they were overworked. The crown prince suggested that the women be divided into three work shifts as a solution.[56] Such a record indicates that the women were, at the very least, working in two shifts, or, more likely, were on duty all day and night. While the number of women serving at the royal palaces increased, it is not clear if such an ideal working environment was achieved, but it is thought that the women were largely divided into the two groups of left and right (*chwa; u*) for most of the dynasty.[57]

For most palace women, the major event in their lives was the coming-of-age ceremony (*kyerye*). Kim Yongsuk states that the general rule was to observe this about fifteen years after the women entered the palace; for girls who entered the palace at four or five years of age, the ceremony would occur when they reached their late teens.[58] For those women who entered the palace at older ages, the ceremony would have been held in less than fifteen years, as the general principle for the *kyerye* in Chosŏn was to hold it in conjunction with a woman's marriage, which normally took place in her mid-to late teens. This ceremony was one of the four great life rituals of upper-status-group families in Chosŏn,[59] although it was normally combined with a woman's marriage in most cases. Most of the palace women, however, would not have the opportunity for marriage, and thus this ritual marked the achievement of adulthood and was conducted with all the flair of a marriage ceremony.[60] As noted above, the major portion of the expenses for this ceremony was borne by the woman's natal home. It was after this ceremony that the woman would begin to work at the palace more or less independent of her former teacher.

---

55 Ch'oe and Ha, *Han'guk yŏsŏng sa*, 513.

56 *T'aejong sillok* [Veritable records of King T'aejong], 27:39a (1414-06-06).

57 Ch'oe and Ha, *Han'guk yŏsŏng sa*, 514.

58 *Chosŏnjo kungjung p'ungsok yŏn'gu*, 40.

59 Coming-of-age, marriage, funerary, and ancestor rites.

60 Kim Yongsuk, *Chosŏnjo kungjung p'ungsok yŏn'gu*, 41.

In most instances, palace women were not allowed to leave the palace or be freed from their status. If one became too old to work or suffered from a disease, she would usually be sent back to her natal home.[61] In the event of a death in her immediate family, a woman would be temporarily released from her duties at the palace for the proper observance of mourning rites. Needless to say, when a palace woman was away from the palace she was not free to act as she wished. Legal codes ensured that those violating the exclusive rights to these women would be punished severely. For keeping a palace woman or palace servant as a concubine, the penalty was one hundred strokes with a cudgel.[62] Of course, the punishment for the woman was much worse: a royal edict in 1667 called for immediate beheading of the culprit.[63]

The greatest sacrifice that the palace women were forced to endure might well have been the inability to have a satisfactory love relationship. Palace women were sometimes selected for sexual relations by their master and subsequently elevated in rank. However, given the large number of women serving a given prince or king, not all would ever realize such a diversion. The understanding of a palace woman's bitterness was widespread as seen in a special term, *yŏwŏn* (woman's rancor), for this plight.[64] Moreover, the simple act of a sexual union with their master does not imply physical or emotional satisfaction for the women.

The emotional difficulties facing palace women because of their forced celibacy is also evident in records acknowledging that the women oftentimes had sexual relations with other women. Such relationships were a matter of personal choice among the women and carried out without regard to status at the palace, with the primary motivation being loneliness.[65] There was also tacit sanction of these relationships as seen in an entry in the dynastic record from 1504.[66] Kim Yongsuk further notes that there was

[61] Ibid., 45.

[62] *Kyŏngguk taejŏn,* 5:7a. See also the 1542 legal code *Taejŏn-hu sok-rok* [Comprehensive later national code, supplemented], 5:8a–8b.

[63] *Sugyo chimnok* [Compilation of royal edicts], 158. A subsequent legal code promulgated in 1746 called for the immediate beheading of both parties. See *Sok tae-jŏn,* 5:27b.

[64] Yi Sun'gu "Chosŏn sidae ŭi sŏngnihak kwa yŏsŏng," 214.

[65] Kim Yongsuk mentions an instance during the reign of Kojong (1864–1907) where a high-ranking *sanggung* palace woman shared quarters with another palace woman who worked as a cook. See *Chosŏnjo kungjung p'ungsok yŏn'gu,* 73.

[66] *Yŏnsan-gun ilgi* [Diary of Prince Yŏnsan], 56:15b (1504-11-08).

even a special term—*taesik* (taking meals together)—for those palace women living as a couple within the royal palace.[67]

Notwithstanding the heavy penalties palace women were subjected to for infidelity, there seem to have been many such cases over the course of the Chosŏn dynasty. Sometimes the accused were spared death in a moment of generosity by the king as seen in the following account reported to the throne by the Office of the Inspector-General (Sahŏnbu):

> "Yi Yŏngnim committed adultery with a serving woman who came out of the palace. According to the codes, we request that they suffer decapitation." The King, however, displayed his generosity by reducing each of their ranks by two.[68]

Other women were not so fortunate. While the dynastic records rarely tell of the death of a palace woman accused of adultery, the omission of any mention of punishment to the female party in the numerous accounts of illicit affairs between men and palace women would seem to indicate that punishment for the guilty woman was a given and needed no debate.[69] Additionally, the legal codes of Chosŏn spelled out in no uncertain terms the punishment for the palace woman guilty of such an offense. From this, we can surmise that a benevolent monarch's sparing of a guilty woman's life was worthy of notation in the dynastic annals.

In the narrative of *Unyŏng-jŏn* we find several instances where the importance of emotional fulfillment for the young palace women is mentioned. This fictional description seems to reflect the actualities of the difficulties in life for the palace women. In the following excerpt spoken by one of Unyŏng's fellow palace women, we can witness the inner turmoil at a life of unnatural isolation:

> However, while being confined resolutely in the deep palace like a bird in a bamboo cage, I lament at the sound of a golden oriole's song and even sob at the [sight of a] green willow. All the worse, I feel so lonely to see even swallows flying in pairs or dozing birds

---

[67] *Chosŏnjo kungjung p'ungsok yŏn'gu*, 73.

[68] *Sejong sillok*, 85:33a (1439-05-15).

[69] There are numerous accounts of the debate for punishment for the male perpetrator of illicit sexual relations with palace women. For example, see *Chungjong sillok* [Veritable records of King Chungjong], 27:11a–11b (1517-11-18), 27:14a (1517-11-22), 27:14b (1517-12-26), and 27:15a (1517-12-27) for a discussion of the appropriate punishment for one Nam Ch'iwŏn, who was charged with such a crime. Despite the numerous entries on his punishment, there is no mention of what happened to the woman.

> roosting face to face. Among the grasses, there are those that intertwine, and among trees, there are those that join roots.[70] Even ignorant grasses and trees and lowly birds have the joy of innate yin and yang. What sin have the ten of us alone committed that we must be fettered to this isolated and lonely palace, while the spring flowers and autumn moon pass? Always oppressed by false rules: why are we destined to such a cruel fate? As once a person is old he or she can never again be young, think again, how can I not be sad![71]

Such a passage as the above is common in the narrative. The reader can clearly understand the emptiness of these women's lives as they see their youth pass. A reoccurring theme of the loneliness described by the women is the unjust nature of such deprivation. Particularly in this aspect, *Unyŏng-jŏn* well depicts the lives of isolation and loneliness suffered by palace women.

The palace women of *Unyŏng-jŏn,* however, do not accurately represent the lives of palace women in other aspects. Particularly, their lives of scholarship and the pursuit of learning does not match the actual circumstances of palace women's lives. Palace women in Chosŏn had specific duties to carry out, and while some might have led lives more comfortable than others, it is doubtful that the vast majority of these women had the opportunity to spend their days writing poetry and debating the classics. Thus the portrayal of this aspect in *Unyŏng-jŏn* is inaccurate as it idealizes the actual working conditions of women in service of the royal palace.

---

[70] This joining of the roots of two trees (*yŏlli*) is a symbol of deep love between husband and wife.

[71] *Unyŏng-jŏn,* 30.

CHAPTER THREE

Unyŏng-jŏn: An Analysis of a Seventeenth-century Novel

While the original edition of *Unyŏng-jŏn* is no longer thought to be extant, numerous copies have been preserved. Despite the lack of the original, we can state with authority that the work was originally written in literary Chinese and then later "translated" into Korean script. Moreover, while there are various versions of *Unyŏng-jŏn,* these are largely the same and hold only minor variations. The work is also known by different titles, a common feature of premodern Korean novels.

The text

Considering the stylistic sophistication of the versions of *Unyŏng-jŏn* written in literary Chinese, we can logically surmise that these versions are the original form of the novel.[1] So Chaeyong writes that while the versions in literary Chinese have some minor differences in regard to the degree of elaboration in some passages and use of homonyms in places, they are largely the same. The hangul renditions, on the other hand, demonstrate a much lower level of literary sophistication as manifested in less artfully wrought descriptions and numerous errors.[2]

To such a stance, we should also add that the poetic forms that abound in *Unyŏng-jŏn* are uniformly forms written exclusively in literary Chinese (*hansi*). Such poems, utilizing *hansi* forms such as seven-character quatrains (*ch'irŏn chŏlgu*), simply could not have been initially written in hangul, which does not allow for such brevity and further cannot match the required form. The frequent

---

[1] Such a stance is supported by numerous scholars. See Pak T'aesang, *Chosŏnjo aejŏng sosŏl yŏn'gu,* 353; Cho Tongil, *Han'guk munhak t'ongsa,* 3:493.

[2] So Chaeyong, "*Unyŏng-jŏn* yŏn'gu," 154–158.

use of such poems throughout the text provides additional solid evidence that the work initially was composed in literary Chinese.

The *hansi* poems in *Unyŏng-jŏn* are further written in Tang-style poetry, reflecting the shift in the mid-Chosŏn period away from Song-style poetry. While Song-style poetry had been in vogue from the late Koryŏ period, by the late sixteenth century Tang-style *hansi* poetry had become prominent. The presence of Tang-style poems in *Unyŏng-jŏn* demonstrates that the writer of the novel was aware of changes in the literary current of the day; moreover, it provides a clue as to the period in which the work was composed.

The immense body of Chinese literature directly referred to or alluded to in *Unyŏng-jŏn* demonstrates a writer well in tune with Chinese literary traditions. Such an individual would not have been inclined to write in a form such as hangul, which was held as inherently inferior. Yet, noting that *Unyŏng-jŏn* was translated into hangul during the seventeenth century, we can understand that some individuals recognized that hangul allowed greater access to literary works. Kim Hŭnggyu cites this as an indicator of the "symbiotic relationship between the two modes of writing."[3] The translation of this work also indicates its popularity among the chief consumer group of hangul novels, that being upper-status-group women.

Notwithstanding the fact that the hangul renditions of *Unyŏng-jŏn* are in some ways inferior when compared to those in literary Chinese, aspects of the hangul versions reveal other elements of interest. Pak Kisŏk writes that the hangul versions of *Unyŏng-jŏn* are the result of a shift in readership of the work from men to women, and over time the hangul versions of the novel came to move toward a female readership. The narrative of the hangul versions places more emphasis on the actions of the palace women and the relationship between Unyŏng and Kim *chinsa* than is present in the versions written in literary Chinese.[4] Such a transformation of the work was no doubt accelerated in the mid to late eighteenth century when the lending of books for profit became common, and works for women became a major component of the book trade.[5]

[3] Kim Hŭnggyu, "Chosŏn Fiction in Chinese," 265.

[4] Pak Kisŏk, "*Unyŏng-jŏn*," 713, quoted in Cho Hŭiung, *Kojŏn sosŏl ibon mongnok*, 452.

[5] The growth of the publishing industry in late Chosŏn was fostered by various factors including a realization of the value of hangul novels as a form of entertainment for those of the lower classes and women. The so-called *panggak-pon*, that is,

The translation in this volume is from two nearly identical versions in literary Chinese. The first is a handwritten copy held at the Changsŏ-gak Library (the former private library of the Chosŏn dynasty's royal family) at the Academy of Korean Studies. This copy bears no date or seal. The second, also a handwritten copy, is held in the Asami Library of the University of California at Berkeley. This copy bears the seal of Yi Kyojin, who once served as magistrate (*kunsu*) of Imch'on.[6] The back cover of this copy is inscribed "Copied on a rainy day, seventh month, *ŭlhae* year." *Ŭlhae* years fell in 1649, 1709, 1769, 1839, and 1899. Additionally, a translation into modern Korean by Yi Sanggu of the handwritten copy in literary Chinese of the work held by the National Library of Korea was consulted at times to ensure accuracy with problematic passages.[7] This same work was also valuable as a reference work as the annotations by Yi oftentimes provided clarification for many historical personages and events.

Titles of the Work

Like many other premodern literary works, *Unyŏng-jŏn* is known by various titles. While *Unyŏng-jŏn* is the most common title, alternative titles include *Susŏng-gung mongyu-rok* [Dream record of Susŏng Palace] and *Yu Yŏng-jŏn* [The tale of Yu Yŏng].[8] The first of these appellations indicates both the location of the narrative and the literary genre used, while the latter refers to the scholar who is said to have met the ghostly Unyŏng and Kim *chinsa* and been given the written story. The novel is further bound together with other works (*happon*), indicating that it was popularly circulated with other fiction. The Asami version used in this translation, for example, is bound together with a ghost story titled *Nogŭi in-jŏn* [The tale of the person in green].

---

works published for commercial purposes, became widespread by the mid-nineteenth century, and a major section of this market was hangul novels aimed at women readers. For further discussion of these works, see Pu Kilman, *Chosŏn sidae paggak-pon ch'ulp'an yŏn'gu*, 96–100.

[6] Chaoying Fang, *The Asami Library: A Descriptive Catalogue*, 276.

[7] Yi Sanggu, *17 segi aejŏng chŏn'gi sosŏl.*

[8] For a full listing of titles, see Cho Hŭiung, *Kojŏn sosŏl ipon mongnok*, 453–455.

Date and Authorship

Because *Unyŏng-jŏn* is not signed by its author, trying both to establish a date of composition and identify the creator of the text is a problem. Most scholars put the creation date of the novel somewhere in the period between 1616 and 1641. The earlier date is based on changes in the characters used for Susŏng Palace, where the narrative unfolds. The characters for Susŏng found in the text were used beginning in 1616, the ninth year of the reign of Kwanghae-gun.[9] The latter date is based upon a copy of the work that bears the date 1641 on its cover.[10] Also providing an upper limit to the creation date is the place name T'angch'un-dae, where the palace women are said to normally do laundry. The name of this location was changed to Yŏnyung-dae in 1754 by royal order.[11]

Other textual evidence, such as accounts of the destruction of the Japanese invasions of 1592–1598 at the beginning of the novel, tends to confirm that the work was created in the early seventeenth century. Moreover, as mentioned above, the presence of Tang-style poetry in the work indicates a creation date no earlier than the end of the sixteenth century. With such evidence in hand, we can safely surmise that the work was created in the early seventeenth century.

The question of authorship is an intriguing one. While it is commonly assumed that this work is that of an upper-status man, the woman-centered descriptions of the lives of palace women and the first-person female narrative voice that dominates the story could indicate otherwise. Is it possible that this literary work of extremely high quality was written by a woman? This question merits a thorough examination.

The assumption that the creator of this work was male is largely based on the fact that it is written in literary Chinese by a writer with a great depth of knowledge in literary traditions. Some scholars have suggested the writer to be none other than the historical Yu Yŏng (1553–1616), the scholar who meets Unyŏng and Kim in the narrative.[12] Yet Yu's own history reveals nothing to suggest that he was an individual of great literary talent. Thus,

[9] Chŏng Ch'urhŏn et al., *Kojŏn munhak kwa yŏsŏngjuŭi-jŏk sigak,* 119.

[10] *Taemyŏng ch'ŏn'gye isipil-nyŏn.*

[11] *Yŏngo sillok* [Veritable records of King Yŏngo], 82:16b (1754-09-02).

[12] Chŏng Kyubok, "*Unyŏng-jŏn* ŭi munje," 115–124.

it is highly doubtful that the writer of such a polished work could have been an uninspiring scholar such as Yu.

The structure and narrative style of the work also demonstrate a significant break from previous literary works of Chosŏn. Kim Kyŏngmi points out that this novel "reveals women's space, desire, and self-awareness" and that this is not told from a male viewpoint.[13] Such qualities of the work indicate a writer with both great knowledge of and empathy concerning the lives of women in general and an understanding of the particular hardships that confronted palace women. Yet to this one should add that the descriptions of the palace women's lives in the narrative seem idealized especially in regard to their very scholarly activities.

Who could such a writer have been? Perhaps an upper-status man who had a relationship with a palace woman similar to that described in *Unyŏng-jŏn*? This is an intriguing possibility and could account for some of the insight the writer had into the lives of these women. That the work is not signed also would support such a viewpoint, as the writer would be wary of the inevitable wrath such a violation of propriety would bring about.

The fact that we can find records of palace women who had love affairs with men outside the palace might support the above hypothesis. As mentioned in chapter 2, there are numerous records of upper-status men having affairs with palace women. Such a relationship would certainly provide a male author with an understanding of life for palace women within the royal palace. Yet even a writer with such a background would not necessarily be entirely aware of how women lived and interacted in the palace. This lack of awareness could account for the rather one-sided understanding of women's lives in terms of service and duties. Moreover, a man's views of women and sexuality would most likely be from a male viewpoint and not provide the female narrative voice and worldview of the writer of *Unyŏng-jŏn*.

Thus, we cannot summarily dismiss the possibility that the writer of this novel was a woman, and most likely, a woman fairly close to the royal court. The narrative voice of the novel—first-person female for the most part—indicates a speaker thoroughly acquainted with women's lives in this period. Even more important, the manner in which the narrative depicts female space and lives is groundbreaking in Chosŏn-period fiction in that it does so from a woman's view. While we do have fiction and poems

---

[13] Kim Kyŏngmi, "*Unyŏng-jŏn*-e nat'anan yŏsŏng sŏsulja ŭi ŭiŭi," 35.

written by men from a feminine viewpoint, these works differ from *Unyŏng-jŏn* in that the predominant worldview is male-centered. There were women in the Chosŏn period who had both access to knowledge and the resources to write such a work. It is too simplistic to merely dismiss this possibility because women are not thought capable of such work.

It should be mentioned that women in the Chosŏn period did excel at various literary forms when given the opportunity. The acclaimed poet Hŏ Nansŏrhŏn (1562–1590) created *hansi* poems of such excellence that they were published and achieved fame in China.[14] Also of note is the didactic writing of Queen Sohye (1437–1504), *Naehun* [Instructions for the inner quarters], and the scholarly exegeses of the Confucian scholars Im Yunjidang (1721–1793) and Kang Chŏnildang (1772–1832). *Pyŏngja ilgi* [A diary of the year *pyŏngja* (i.e., 1636)] is a diary kept by Lady Cho of Namp'yŏng (1574–1645) for a period extending from the end of 1636 though the eighth lunar month of 1640 and is one of the best records of daily life of upper-status families during the Manchu invasions. Additionally, the autobiography of Lady Hong of Hyegyŏng Palace (1734–1815), *Hanjung-rok* [Record of sorrowful days], is acclaimed for the writing skills of the author. Coupled with the writings of known authors is the immense body of literature—including both poetry and novels—that is thought to be the work of women. For example, there are numerous *kyubang* novels (novels of the women's quarters) previously attributed to unknown men that scholars now believe to have been written by women.[15]

Yet the lives of the women in this novel are not entirely accurate portrayals of how palace women of this period would have lived. A palace woman probably would not have presented such an idealized model of life, especially in the aspect of Grand Prince Anp'yŏng's allowing these ten women to devote their lives to study. While palace women had opportunity for education, they did not lead lives as scholars reading and debating poetry. Rather, they worked long hours at specific duties. Thus, it does not seem likely that this is the work of a palace woman.

A close reading of *Unyŏng-jŏn* displays several features that support the possibility that this is a text written by a woman.[16]

[14] For more on Hŏ Nasŏrhŏn, see Hŏ Mija, *Han'guk yŏsŏng munhak yŏn'gu*, 83–100.

[15] See Chŏng Ch'urhŏn, *Kojŏn sosŏlsa ŭi kudu wa sigak*, 189–215.

[16] I am indebted to JaHyun Kim Haboush's examination of the authorship of

First, the work is imbued with an undeniable sympathy for the difficulties and powerlessness of women. Male-authored texts have been argued to present images of relationships between women primarily in terms of sexual rivalry and betrayal.[17] This is seen to a certain degree in male-authored novels such as *Sassi namjŏnggi* [A record of Lady Sa's trip to the south] and *Ch'angsŏn kamŭi-rok* [That goodness be manifest and righteousness prized].[18]

Unyŏng-jŏn, while not altogether absent of discord among women, instead highlights the comradeship and affinity of the palace women. Their hardships are clearly depicted, and the reader is privy to their deepest thoughts concerning both their physical and mental confinement. While the women are divided into two groups by the Grand Prince and experience initial conflicts, they overcome this artificial separation—imposed by a man—and eventually act with a single accord. Though Unyŏng alone shatters the bonds of emotional and physical thralldom, her comrades echo her discontent at an unnatural life. By the work's conclusion Unyŏng demonstrates autonomy through her choice to commit suicide rather than live in captivity at the royal palace.

Further notable is that Unyŏng is not presented as a morally inadequate woman, despite her affair with Kim, which is a clear breach of Confucian propriety. If the narrative were told from a male perspective, one could envision that Unyŏng would be a less proactive character; she would not be the initiator of the affair with Kim, she would not be the one to end the meetings, and she would not be such a morally superior character. However, few women were allowed to tell their own stories in Korean fiction; rather, we learn of women's lives through male perceptions and standards.[19] This work thus demonstrates very clear understanding of and support and sympathy for a woman's life, quite unlike most male-authored texts.

Inhyŏn wanghu-jŏn for the structure of my argument concerning the writer of *Unyŏng-jŏn*. Not surprisingly, many of the same qualities are found in the two works that seem to have been written by women. See JaHyun Kim Haboush, "Versions and Subversions: Patriarchy and Polygamy in Korean Narratives," 290–292.

[17] Pam Morris, *Literature and Feminism*, 61.

[18] *Sassi namjŏnggi* is the work of Kim Manjung (1637–1692) and highlights the competition between a wife and a concubine. *Ch'angsŏn kamŭi-rok* is thought to have been written by Cho Sŏnggi (1638–1689) and centers on the discord among wives.

[19] A similar situation has been noted in Qing literature. See Martin W. Huang, *Desire and Fictional Narrative in Late Imperial China*, 126–129.

Second, *Unyŏng-jŏn* features a protagonist who is certainly superior to the men in the text not only in terms of morality, but also in autonomy. Unyŏng does not see her love affair with Kim to be a violation of any ethic: she does not recognize the social system that holds her captive in the palace, nor does she see herself as being the possession of Anp'yŏng. She does not enter into a relationship with Anp'yŏng either, as her heart is not set upon him and she respects his wife as she does her own mother. If we consider this aspect of the narrative from a woman's viewpoint, it could indicate a desire by women to be free of the concubinage system, which pitted women against each other in competition for a man's favors. She terminates the affair with Kim upon realizing that continuing would endanger her fellow palace women. Unyŏng is a highly principled woman who lives according to her own understanding of morality and does not waver from this position. Her upright character and morality are in stark contrast to the characters of the corrupt men portrayed in the work including Anp'yŏng, the slave T'ŭk, and to a lesser degree, Kim *chinsa.*

In terms of agency, we can also see that Unyŏng is able to take control of her own destiny to a greater degree than the other characters. She realizes her heart's desire in meeting Kim and is able to share love with him. At the same time, she rejects a possible physical relationship with Anp'yŏng. Her death is also of her own choice. The character thus represents a woman in control of her own life, despite the unfavorable conditions in which she must live.

Such characteristics of Unyŏng and other characters in this work display a clear break from standard markers of male-authored texts. In many works by male writers we can note indulgence in male fantasies on one hand, and on the other, the repression of female characters who challenge the patriarchal system.[20] In *Unyŏng-jŏn,* however, the female protagonist does not follow such a pattern: Unyŏng is an autonomous character of great emotional strength, and even in death she presents a dignified and principled character. Such an image must have been both extremely popular among women readers and a source of inspiration, at least as a proxy for their own lives.

Thus, it is not correct to dismiss the possibility of a female author for a work such as *Unyŏng-jŏn* simply based on stereotypical notions of what women were not capable of in the Chosŏn

[20] Pam Morris, *Literature and Feminism,* 39.

dynasty. I think that the narrative of *Unyŏng-jŏn* clearly reveals an author unlike any heretofore seen in early- to mid-Chosŏn fiction and one with more than passing knowledge of and empathy for a woman's life in the royal palace. The worldview of this writer is also unique in that the narrative unfolds from a woman's perspective and emotions. Hence, it is more than plausible that the writer of this work was a woman.

The Dream Record

The structure of *Unyŏng-jŏn* is centered on a common literary device in premodern Korean and East Asian literature known as a "dream record" (K. *mongyu-rok,* C. *mengliu-lu*). In this genre, the narrative unfolds as a ghostly narrator retells a story of past days to an individual of the present age or as an individual of this world travels to the next through the medium of a dream. This form was popular in early Korean fiction because it allowed writers to expand the limitations of the mundane world.

The actual use of a dream record dates to some of the oldest Korean fiction. Recorded in the *Samguk yusa* [Memorabilia of the Three Kingdoms, 1285] is the tale of Chosin, a short narrative that reveals perhaps the first Korean use of such a structure.[21] The Koryŏ period literatus Yi Kyubo (1168–1241) also uses this form in a first-person narrative about his own dream journey in *Paegun sosŏl* [Short essays by Paegun].[22] The use of this form in what we can term a novel, however, would have to wait until the early Chosŏn writer Kim Sisŭp (1435–1493) and his *Kŭmo sinhwa* [New tales from Mt. Golden Turtle]. This work contains five short narratives, and all employ the use of a dream-record encounter to some degree.

The prototypical model of a dream-record narrative is *Wŏnsaeng mongnyu-rok* [Dream record of Master Wŏn, 1568], most likely written by Im Che (1549–1587). In this work, we can note the first use of the dream record as a tool for social criticism, which would become the most common future use of this genre. This particular work is a forum to criticize the usurpation of the throne by King Sejo (r. 1455–1468) in 1455; it features a dream sequence where the protagonist, Wŏn Chahŏ, a righteous scholar, attends a meeting of the deposed king, Tanjong (r. 1452–1455),

21 Iryŏn, *Samguk yusa*, 322–330.

22 Yi Kyubo, *Paegun sosŏl* [Short essays by Paegun], 25–30.

and the so-called six martyred ministers (*sayuksin*) who went to their deaths for criticizing the usurpation.[23] In exposing the accusations against the deceased king and ministers as being false, the work takes a decidedly dangerous position, strongly critical of Sejo's usurpation. The dream journey, however, provided a safer space for such a commentary.

The dream record form became a common structural device for the *chŏn'gi* (tales of wonder) novels of the early to middle Chosŏn period. In addition to allowing criticism, the form also permitted more freedom in plot development through the use of supernatural entities, reexamining historical events and personages, and juxtaposing the real and fictional worlds. Works in this genre include *Kuun-mong* [Dream of nine clouds] and *Ongmu-mong* [Dream of the jade pavilion] among numerous others.

The reasons for the popularity of this genre bear closer inspection. One view in general of ghosts in fiction is that they are reflective of a desire to "aid human affairs by restoring justice and moral order."[24] We can see this aspect in narratives such as *Wŏnsaeng mongnyu-rok*, which criticizes what the author saw as an unjust political situation. Yet ghosts in other fictional works do not always embody this concept of "restoring justice and moral order." For example, in Kim Sisŭp's *Kŭmo sinhwa* we find narratives that reflect much more personal ghosts, entities that have what can be said to be very individual reasons for remaining among the living. In "Yi saeng kujang-jŏn" [Student Yi peers over the wall] we see a ghost that clings to this world because of her love for her husband. After death at the hand of the Red Turban bandits, the wife returns to her husband as a ghost. They live together for three years as husband and wife before she informs him that she must move on to the next world. She asks her husband to bury her remains, which had yet not been properly interned, and shortly after doing so, he dies.[25] Other early-Chosŏn-period narratives echo such individual reasons for ghosts' remaining in or visiting this world.[26]

---

[23] These men were Yi Kae, Ha Wiji, Yu Sŏngwŏn, Yu Ŭngbu, Sŏng Sammun, and Pak P'aengnyŏn.

[24] Rosemary Jackson, *Fantasy: The Literature of Subversion*, 97.

[25] Recorded in Kim Sisŭp, *Kŭmo sinhwa*, 98–133.

[26] In *Kŭmo sinhwa*, another narrative "Manboksa chŏp'o-ki" [Record of playing chŏp'o at Manbok Temple], features a woman killed by bandits whose ghost returns to this world and shares poetry and love with a scholar.

Narratives such as the above seem to convey the notion that ghostly beings can overturn injustices, be they political or individual. Perhaps this function is best explained in terms of the relative latitude that an otherworldly narrator has for social criticism. Rather than stating the direct critique of a writer, these fictional works use the voice of the dead. This can be a means to question "the moral fitness of the living or the agency responsible" for a death.[27] Thus, one function of the ghost and the dream record is to bring to light the inadequacies of ruling systems and social values that contributed to unjust deaths.

Yet fictional narratives of ghosts are not simply social critiques. More than subversive diatribes of hegemonic systems, these narratives are also revealing of how writers, and perhaps readers too, viewed the next world. The idea of the dead speaking to the living is one deeply embedded in premodern Korea through the practices of shamanic rituals where spirits speak through a shaman. Indeed, the ghost of one who has died with bitterness or a grudge (*han*) is the most feared ghost in popular folk beliefs as it is thought that this spirit will not leave the human world until its dissatisfaction is resolved. We can logically extend this to the return of ghosts to fulfill earthly desires, be these yearnings for love or revenge, or simply to tell their story of a social wrong.

Unyŏng-jŏn unfolds from such an encounter between the living and the dead. A maladroit scholar, Yu Yŏng, decides that he will finally take in the beauty of Inwang Mountain and alone heads up the mountain. Such an individual as Yu is necessary for the narrative to progress. Without such a pure-minded yet socially disconnected scholar, there could be no encounter between the secular and sacred worlds. Yu being pure of heart and free from both political and social encumbrances is thus able to transcend the strict boundary between this world and the next. In fact, his "otherness" is a point for ridicule when others see him, as "there was not a single occasion when they did not point and laugh."[28]

Such an individual is the only one who possesses the prerequisite sincerity needed to bond with the pitiful ghosts that he would soon encounter. Yu has a true heart, one not fettered by worldly desires or greed. He matches the model established by

[27] JaHyun Kim Haboush, "Dead Bodies in the Postwar Discourse of Identity in Seventeenth-Century Korea: Subversion and Literary Production in the Private Sector," 422–423.

[28] *Unyŏng-jŏn*, 2.

the protagonist of *Wŏn-saeng mongnyu-rok* and also the protagonists in the tales recorded in *Kŭmo sinhwa*. As a righteous scholar, he is trusted by those of the next world who can clearly see into the human condition. His upright character makes him the ideal human to transmit this story to, and also one who can be trusted to relay the message of the storytellers without deviation.

In *Unyŏng-jŏn* we see criticism of items such as the gender bias that held women inherently inferior to men, of the social system that did not grant freedom of choice, of the bonds that held some individuals in perpetual servitude to those of the highest classes, and of restrictions placed on following one's heart in matters as basic as love. For a writer to criticize these institutions outright, he or she would face certain censure and perhaps a heavy penalty under the legal codes of the day. Certainly, the writer of *Unyŏng-jŏn* was aware of the possibility of punishment for the social critique contained in this work, and thus the work does not bear the author's name. This was a first line of defense to prevent punishment for the controversial views in the work.

In addition to writing anonymously, the author, as a second line of defense, further incorporated an otherworldly storyteller. The ghosts of Unyŏng and Kim provide much greater latitude for a social critique on Chosŏn society. Beings of the next world are not bound by the rules of the profane world. Moreover, Unyŏng and Kim are heavenly beings, as the narrative tells that they serve the Jade Emperor in the heavenly palace. As such, they are not only free from the conventional rules that bond humans, but they are imbued further with the protection and virtue of the Jade Emperor. This allows them special privilege to impart a moral message to their audience.

The past lives of these storytellers also create a line of defense. Their lives ended some 150 years before the actual retelling of their story. Accordingly, they are not criticizing the present court or elites, but rather quite distant ancestors. Of course, this too was dangerous, but not nearly as much as criticizing the present age or the near past.

The meeting of the three main characters takes place in the environs of the old grounds of Prince Anp'yŏng's residence, Susŏng Palace. Notable is the ruin of the palace, destroyed in the Japanese invasions of 1592–1598, and its isolation from the capital city below. The setting of the palace, itself a ghostly ruins, provides the ideal location for a meeting of the supernatural and the profane worlds.

While the otherworldly qualities of Unyŏng and Kim seem obvious in the narrative, those qualities appear not to surprise Yu. Rather, his curiosity at the origins of Unyŏng's and Kim's distress drives him to press the couple for details on their lives. The two are not immediately ready to open old wounds, yet at Yu's pressing Unyŏng reluctantly agrees to tell their story. It is thus Yu, in the midst of his dream, who seems to initiates this exchange.

Notwithstanding that Yu is the one who prods the couple to tell their story, we can surmise that this was the wish of the couple from the outset. Although Yu wandered into their meeting after hearing their conversation, the couple warmly greeted him and asked him to join their company. Moreover, Unyŏng does not simply *tell* her story to Yu. Rather, she summons her maidservant to bring her a writing brush, inkstone, and paper, and records the narrative. Finally, at the conclusion of the storytelling, Kim entreats Yu to pass on their words by means of the manuscript, telling him, "Dear Sir, please take this writing and pass it on to the world for the ages. Moreover, please keep this from frivolous people who speak indiscriminately and take it trifling. All I wish is that you do as such."[29] It is clear that the couple intended to meet Yu and use him to relay their story to those of the present age. The reader is now treated to the story of the love between Unyŏng and Kim.

Placing *Unyŏng-jŏn* in the larger context of Korean dream literature, we can note some of the same chords of social critique that are seen in *Wŏn-saeng mongnyu-rok.* Of course, in the latter work the criticism is politically oriented whereas in the former it is directed more toward voicing dissatisfaction with concerns in women's lives such as lack of freedom of choice and subordination to men in general. We can also see a clear questioning of the political and social system that led to the death of Unyŏng and the morality of those who supported this system. In this aspect, *Unyŏng-jŏn* is a highly disparaging discourse on the social, political, and cultural systems of Chosŏn.

Like most other works in the dream-record genre, *Unyŏng-jŏn* features lengthy debates and conversations in which a certain viewpoint or activity is justified. We can note such discourse when the women debate where to do the laundry, the character of Unyŏng, and ultimately, when they present petitions to the Grand Prince before Unyŏng's death. The author's critiques of the

---

[29] *Unyŏng-jŏn,* 66.

Chosŏn social system are most vivid at these points in the narrative, as the writer uses the debate among the women as a means to clearly bring into question the oppressive structures that limit the personal freedoms of the women. Much like a debate before the king in the court, the women take turns outlining lucid arguments of their critiques of a social system that denied them basic autonomy. It is at the points of these discussions that the reader would have been indoctrinated into alternative modes of thinking.

Through the ghostly narrators, the writer of this work attempts to subvert the hegemonic cultural structures of the day and demonstrate that other possibilities exist for a more just and moral society. The dream record provides a perfect vehicle for such a critique.

Grand Prince Anp'yŏng

One character in this narrative who actually graces the pages of Korean history is Grand Prince Anp'yŏng. Anp'yŏng was the third son of King Sejong (r. 1418–1450) and said to have been an accomplished poet and calligrapher. A near contemporary of Anp'yŏng, Sŏng Hyŏn (1439–1504), described the prince as

> excelling at scholarship and poetry, and his skills at calligraphy were unmatched by any....He always drank and bantered joyfully, and for any reason he would engage in discussions with the famous Confucian scholars of the day; also in his following was a large group of scoundrels.[30]

Perhaps befitting the son of Sejong, Anp'yŏng was highly interested in scholarship and enjoyed the refined culture of his day. And not unlike other members of the royal family, he also realized the value of having followers to do his dirty work in trying to realize his political ambitions.

Anp'yŏng was, however, the loser in a political struggle with his brother Grand Prince Suyang (King Sejo, r. 1455–1468). Anp'yŏng allied himself with civil-officials such as Kim Chongsŏ (1390–1453) and Hwangbo In (?-1453) in his clash with his elder brother Suyang, the second son of Sejong, for the kingship. The relationship between the brothers became increasingly contentious after the death of their father and during the reign of Sejong's eldest son, King Munjong (r. 1450–1452). Munjong was sickly and

[30] Sŏng Hyŏn, *Yŏngjae ch'onghwa* [Miscellany by Yŏngjae], 2:80–81.

not a strong king. In the last year of his reign, Suyang took control of administering the country. The death of Munjong and the ascension to the throne by his son Tanjong (r. 1452–1455), a boy only twelve years old, exacerbated the tension and led Suyang, assisted primarily by military officials, to seize full control of the country in the Purge of 1453 (Kyeyu chŏngnan). Anp'yŏng was exiled and eventually forced to commit suicide by drinking poison.

An interesting question is why the author of *Unyŏng-jŏn* selected Anp'yŏng for this text. The backdrop to this inclusion is found in the political history of early Chosŏn, in particular the conflict between the Hungup'a and the Sarimp'a. The Hungup'a had supported the foundation of the dynasty and received political positions and economic reward for their aid. Even during the time of Sejong, these men held most of the kingdom's political power. However, after the usurpation by Sejo and in the subsequent reign of Sŏngjong (r. 1469–1494), many more were rewarded for their support, and the ranks of this group swelled. These Hungup'a possessed both political power and economic wealth, and their actions, naturally, sought to preserve this privilege.

Enter the Sarimp'a. Many in this group had remained outside political power from the onset of the dynasty and instead pursued the study of Confucianism. Their view of government and the administration of the country was Confucian and highly idealistic, and thus contrasted greatly with views of the entrenched Hungup'a. When members of this group began to enter the government in force during the reign of Sŏngjong and criticized what they saw as the extravagant and hedonistic lives of the Hungup'a, conflict between the groups came to a head. In a series of literati purges (*sahwa*) over the course of much of the next century, the Hungup'a sought to retain their power by either exiling or executing the Sarim.[31]

We can link this political struggle with the battle between Anp'yŏng and Suyang at least in terms of Anp'yŏng's desire to continue the reforms of his father and Suyang's wishes to seize the kingship. Sejong fostered scholarship outside the traditional avenues of power in the Chiphyŏn-jŏn (Hall of Worthies), an institution through which he wanted to reshape the political structures

[31] For a fuller discussion of this situation see Ki-baik Lee, *A New History of Korea*, 201–209.

of Chosŏn.[32] Anp'yŏng was closely associated with men of this institution such as Sŏng Sammun (1418–1456), and his battles with his brother for political power centered on his desire to continue reforms led by these men. The defeat of Anp'yŏng, then, was a defeat for this group of reformers who sought to reshape early-Chosŏn government. It is notable that Suyang, upon taking the throne, abolished the Chiphyŏn-jŏn.

By the middle-Chosŏn period the Sarimp'a had taken power, but the country was beset by other problems stemming in part from factional politics within this group and the devastation from the Japanese invasions of the late-sixteenth century. Anp'yŏng represented a positive link to the halcyon times of his father, Sejong. His fostering of scholarship in the text, albeit with women, has been linked to his father's creation of the Chiphyŏn-jŏn.[33] Such a connection becomes all the more prominent when we consider that one of the scholars identified as a common visitor with Anp'yŏng in *Unyŏng-jŏn* is none other than Sŏng Sammun, perhaps the most famous of all the Chiphyŏn-jŏn scholars.[34] Certainly for the reader of the seventeenth century, this connection would have conjured up images of Sejong's benevolent reign and that prosperous time. The link with the political struggles of the mid-fifteenth century also would not have been lost on the seventeenth-century reader. When Yu Yŏng first meets Unyŏng and Kim, his interest is piqued at the mere mention of Anp'yŏng: "Tales of the time of Grand Prince Anp'yŏng and the reasons for the sorrow of a *chinsa:* can you tell me of these things in detail?"[35] To readers in the late Chosŏn, the days of Anp'yŏng and his father would have been era loaded with intrigue on one hand and thoughts of a peaceful time on the other.

In *Unyŏng-jŏn* Anp'yŏng is presented as a somewhat enlightened man in that he decides that women are just as capable as men in learning. He thus selects ten of his palace women and

[32] While the Chiphyŏn-jŏn actually predated Sejong, the function of this institution was greatly enhanced by the young king in 1420. The group of young scholars working at the Chiphyŏn-jŏn served the throne by discussing education, legal codes, and administration of the country. Among the many accomplishments by this group is the development of hangul. As this group was outside the traditional power avenues of Chosŏn, the established power elite viewed them as a threat.

[33] See Chŏng Ch'urhŏn, *Kojŏn sosŏlsa ŭi kudu wa sigak*, 94.

[34] Sŏng was also a member of the *sayuksin*, the six scholars who went to their deaths for opposing Sejo's usurpation of the throne.

[35] *Unyŏng-jŏn*, 5.

begins to instruct them in the Confucian Classics and the poetry of the Tang-dynasty masters. The seeming progressive nature of Anp'yŏng is tempered with his strict control of the women, all under the threat of death if they should stray from his flock: "If anyone of you goes outside of the palace gate one time, for that crime she will suffer death. If an outsider knows one of your names, for that crime too you will not escape from death."[36]

The contradictory nature of the Grand Prince bears closer examination. He acknowledges that both men and women are capable of the same level of scholarship and trains his palace women in the same manner that men would have experienced. Starting with the basic Confucian texts, they attain a very high level of knowledge in just five years, demonstrating that women are every bit as capable as men in scholarship. Despite this leaning toward enlightenment, however, Anp'yŏng's manipulative nature demonstrates that he was anything but progressive. First, Anp'yŏng not only taught his fledging flock of scholars, but also controlled their every behavior. The women were confined to isolated parts of Susŏng Palace and not allowed to be seen by the Grand Prince's many visitors. Further, as mentioned above, was the threat of death should they become known to those outside the palace. In addition to these simple physical restraints on the women, there were also psychological fetters. As Chŏng Ch'urhŏn pointed out, Anp'yŏng's practice of evaluating each of the women's poems with reward or punishment reflects a form of ideological censorship.[37] Anp'yŏng employed the poems he ordered the women to write as a means to delve into their psyche, and he used this window as a way to completely dominate and oppress the women.

We can see the level to which Anp'yŏng used this mental manipulation to control the women early in the text. Unyŏng, after her first encounter with Kim, becomes the object of the Grand Prince's suspicion because of a poem she writes at his behest:

In the far-off place, the bluish smoke is a wisp,
The beauty stops weaving silken gauze.[38]

---

[36] *Unyŏng-jŏn*, 8.

[37] *Kojŏn sosŏlsa ŭi kudu wa sigak*, 91.

[38] The beauty weaving silk might be an allusion to Chignyŏ, the woman in the legend of the Weaver Girl and Shepherd Boy (*Kyŏnu-Chignyŏ sŏlhwa*), which dates to the Chinese Zhou dynasty (1027 BCE–771 BCE).

In the wind, alone, disillusioned and sad,
It [the clouds] flies off and falls on Mt. Mu [becoming rain].[39]

Anp'yŏng reads Unyŏng's poem and states that she is obviously yearning for a lover. Her allusions to the beauty who puts aside her weaving harkens forth the legend of the weaver girl who put down her weaving after she met and fell in love with a shepherd boy. Coupled with this well-known legend is Unyŏng's reference to Mt. Mu, famous in poetry for being the locale of heavenly fairies and also often used as a metaphor for a sexual union. While she vehemently denies his charge, the Grand Prince states, "'As poems are what one has in his or her mind, they are not something that can be covered or hidden. Do not say that again.'"[40] The control of the Grand Prince thus extends to the mental level, as the thoughts of his palace women are examined closely and under his sole interpretation. His training of the women was not to develop them fully as distinctive individuals, but rather to mold them into something he alone could possess and enjoy.[41] Chŏng Ch'urhŏn thus sees Susŏng Palace as a grounds for the "formation of human character," although this is done in a very manipulative manner.[42]

Certainly the women realize the control the Grand Prince is exerting on them through their poems. While Unyŏng is the one who is initially accused and subjected to Anp'yŏng's suspicions, she is not the only one who feels the psychological intrusions of the Grand Prince. When Unyŏng is threatened with death near the end of the narrative by the Grand Prince, her close comrade Charan pledges to never again "pick up a brush and write with it."[43] The idea that a poem is a window into one's mind is further strengthened at other spots in the narrative where the poems of the women are analyzed by the Grand Prince and his visitors. We can thus see that Anp'yŏng's control of the palace women extended to the deepest reaches of their minds. Rather than an enlightened master, Anp'yŏng in this text has taken oppression and domination to a new level. Chŏng Ch'urhŏn argues that the fictional Anp'yŏng's desire in *Unyŏng-jŏn* to dominate the women

---

39 *Unyŏng-jŏn*, 10. Musan (C. Wushan) also appears in much Chinese literature as a metaphor for a sexual relationship.

40 *Unyŏng-jŏn*, 11.

41 Chŏng Ch'urhŏn, *Kojŏn sosŏlsa ŭi kudu wa sigak*, 93.

42 Ibid., 91.

43 *Unyŏng-jŏn*, 51.

in the palace is a manifestation of the real-life Anp'yŏng's wish to gain political power.[44]

Any discussion of Anp'yŏng as an enlightened individual who recognized the mental capabilities of women as being on par with men's must further be tempered by the fact that his order sent Unyŏng to her death. Also, the women are isolated from the outside world in the royal palace, and very much treated as playthings to be enjoyed by the Grand Prince at his leisure. The very basic human desires of love, enjoying life, and moving about have all been denied to the women in Anp'yŏng's grasp, and their lives perhaps more closely resemble that of prisoners rather than women living life in luxury.

Unyŏng and the Female Narrator

The character of Unyŏng has been fashioned by the writer of this work to create a figure that readers could easily sympathize with and wish success. Simultaneously a model of innocence and youthful passion, her innocence is captured in her naïveté in attempting to pursue a relationship with Kim, and her passion is revealed in her reckless desire for him. Moreover, she is a window to basic human emotions such as unrequited love, longing for a lover, and steadfast refusal to stray from her hopes. Her emotional appeals to Kim and her fellow palace women are heart-wrenching yet, at the same time, lucid arguments for the realization of basic autonomy.

The character of Unyŏng further embodies the most realistic and fully developed female character in early- to mid-Chosŏn fiction. Unlike female characters in contemporary or even later works, Unyŏng is a multidimensional persona portraying a full range of emotions: this character takes the reader through a gamut of emotions including love, friendship, and endless sorrow. More typical depictions of women include the much more famous female protagonists of late-Chosŏn works such as *Ch'unhyang-jŏn* [The tale of Ch'unhyang] or *Sim Ch'ŏng-jŏn* [The tale of Sim Ch'ŏng], which offer readers a much flatter and one-dimensional portrayal of a woman's life.[45] In such protagonists as these, we

---

[44] *Kojŏn sosŏlsa ŭi kudu wa sigak*, 94–95.

[45] In *Ch'unhyang-jŏn* the overriding trait of the female protagonist is that of fidelity, while the character in *Sim Ch'ŏng-jŏn* is a model of filial piety, both decidedly Confucian traits and representations of women.

cannot see a woman possessing agency and autonomy as is manifested in the character Unyŏng.

Most notable is that this novel is told primarily from Unyŏng's point of view, and thus the reader is allowed to enter a woman's space that is seldom seen in other Chosŏn-period fiction. In fact, *Unyŏng-jŏn* is the first fictional prose in Korean literary history with a female narrator. The reader can experience emotions of isolation, elation, desire, love, and utter heartbreak through the words of a woman, rather than as understood through male characters. The work provides readers with a view of passion and tragedy as told from a woman's viewpoint, providing a very new glimpse of life in Chosŏn.

While the narrative voice of *Unyŏng-jŏn* does shift at times to an omniscient viewpoint, it ultimately returns to Unyŏng's voice and experiences. This aspect is seen in the narrator's use of the humble pronoun *ch'ŏp* (concubine) to refer to herself. This is, without a doubt, the story of Unyŏng and her experiences, told through her own vision.

As Unyŏng's life centered on the very private space allowed to the palace women of Susŏng Palace, this narrative too permits readers to enter this highly restricted space. The reader is privy to the secret thoughts and aspirations of the palace women, along with their emotional distress at leading lives of such isolation. The narrative thus features the lives and emotions of women as understood by a woman. In this aspect, *Unyŏng-jŏn* differs greatly from other early- to mid-Chosŏn fiction, which usually portrays women and women's spaces through male eyes.

In Korean fiction of this period, the reader is most commonly introduced to a woman or a woman's space through the eyes of a male protagonist. Oftentimes, this looking is done secretly by the protagonist. The following passage from *Chu saeng-jŏn* [Tale of Master Chu] is a typical example of a man looking in at women:[46]

> While the house was small, it was exceedingly beautiful. Through a half open gauze blind, a candle shone like daylight. Under the candlelight were the floating movements of women wearing red skirts and blue jackets; it was, just like a picture. Mr. Chu hid himself and while holding his breath, stealthily gazed upon [this scene].[47]

[46] *Chu saeng-jŏn* was written by Kwŏn P'il (1569–1612), most likely in the early seventeenth century. The text examined in this discussion is contained in Yi Sang-gu, *17 segi aejŏng chŏn'gi sosŏl*, 35–67.

In this passage, the women's space is secretly violated by a man, and his glimpses create an exotic and perhaps idealized image of a spot unattainable or prohibited to most men.

Rather than exoticizing the lives of women and where they live, *Unyŏng-jŏn* holds images that show how women viewed the world. The following passage describes the room where Unyŏng and Kim are finally able to come together. Note that this is told from the first-person perspective of Unyŏng:

> I was sitting in my room alone with a gauze window open, a jade lamp brightly lit, a tulip-scented, animal-shaped golden fire pot, and a volume of *Taiping guangji* open on a glass desk in front of me.[48] When I saw him coming in, I rose to greet him and bowed, and he returned my bow and greeting. Like guest and master of the house, we separated and sat on the east and west.[49]

This passage reveals a much more straightforward accounting of the room and its content. While the passage still describes a similar night scene, this time the woman is not objectified as in *Chu saeng-jŏn.*

At other points in *Unyŏng-jŏn,* the reader is treated to views of male spaces through Unyŏng's eyes. In the same manner that the male protagonist spies upon the female space in *Chu saeng-jŏn,* Unyŏng watches the Grand Prince and his guests through a hole in the paper wall. Yet her descriptions are devoid of the ornamentation found in the male accounts of women; instead they are matter-of-fact retellings of the events that transpired.

It is also noteworthy that the descriptions of the women's quarters by Unyŏng are plainer than we see in the example from *Chu saeng-jŏn,* which seems to create a beautiful space for women to occupy. In *Unyŏng-jŏn* readers are treated to descriptions of everyday spaces, where women study, debate, and live, rather than an exotic place of secrets. In the following excerpt, Unyŏng describes the scene after the Grand Prince first suspects her of being unfaithful:

> The ten [of us] all retired to the rooms in the east. There a tall candle was lit, and on a cloisonné desk lay a volume of Tang rhymes. In the volume were the sorrowful poems[50] of palace

---

47 *Chu saeng-jŏn,* 44.

48 *Taiping guangji* [Extensive gleanings of the reign of Great Tranquility] is a Chinese work of fiction compiled by Li Fang in 981.

49 *Unyŏng-jŏn,* 44.

50 These are the *kungwŏn shi,* poems of bitterness and heartbreak written by palace women.

> women, written long ago. The palace women, except for me, debated the merits of these poems. Alone, I leaned against a folding screen, sitting dejectedly and not speaking, like a person made of mud.[51]

Although the trappings of the room befit a royal palace, these are not the focus of the description. Instead, the reader sees that these women are engaged in scholarly debate just like the educated men of the day. The overriding emotion is sorrow and the emptiness of a palace woman's life, but the activity of the women centers on study, the domain of elite men in Chosŏn.

Descriptions of lovemaking in *Unyŏng-jŏn* are in sharp contrast to those in other Chosŏn fiction. Commonly, narratives feature a strong male protagonist who initiates action, oftentimes by overpowering the object of his desires. The following passage from *Chu saeng-jŏn* demonstrates such a scene:

> While deliberately pretending not to hear, Sŏnhwa put out the candle and went to the sleeping mat. Chu entered the room and lay down with Sŏnhwa on the mat. Sŏnhwa was youthful, and her delicate body not yet touched by a man. However, wrapped in a wisp-like cloud with a misty rain, a willow branch quivered, and the flower coquettishly whispered fragrant sobs, her quiet smile distorted. Chu, as a bee covets honey and a butterfly loves flowers, lost his senses to the extent that he did not even realize the break of day.[52]

In this passage, the man takes the initiative in the union although it seems that the woman (i.e., Sŏnhwa) is not opposed to his advances. However, the descriptions of Sŏnhwa depict a virginal and submissive woman, whereas the image of Chu is of a man drunken with an animal lust who falls into an unconscious lovemaking frenzy while devouring his prey.

Similar to this passage is the account found in *Wei Kyŏngch'ŏn-jŏn* [The tale of Wei Kyŏngch'ŏn][53] when the protagonist overcomes the initial protestations of his object of lust:

> The maiden had fallen into a deep spring sleep, and her crimson sleeping gown did not move at all. Wei rolled up his sleeves and entered the room. The maiden was surprised, saying, "Who is this

51 *Unyŏng-jŏn*, 11.

52 *Chu saeng-jŏn*, 50.

53 This work is under the pen name Kwŏn Sŏkchuje, but nothing else is known for certain of this writer. The work is thought to have been written in the early to mid-seventeenth century. The text used in this discussion is the translation into modern Korean in Yi Sanggu, *17 segi aejŏng chŏn'gi sosŏl*, 68–95.

> impudent madman entering this house?" She strongly spurned him, and Wei had no choice but to retire [and leave the room]. However, the door was firmly shut, and the situation was such that there was no way to leave. Wei thought to himself that if such talk were known to his family there would be no other way for him but to die; thus, he was on the verge of taking the maiden by force. The maiden had a somewhat suspicious expression as she considered Wei's words—at times gentle like a gallant youth and at other times harsh like a scoundrel. Thereupon, Wei, in a somewhat low voice, told her that he intended to come close in full detail. The maiden gradually softened her heart [toward him] and little by little, stopped resisting him.[54]

While the woman in this passage does not truly seem opposed to taking a lover, her initial rejection serves to fulfill propriety. That is, a proper woman should not allow a lover in such a situation, and thus she provides token resistance to Wei's first advances. Wei, on the other hand, is driven by his own pride to finish his conquest and continues to press himself upon the woman, eventually realizing his desires.

Unlike such male-centered accounts, *Unyŏng-jŏn* provides both a much more active female participant and a less power-oriented love scene. The love between Unyŏng and Kim is obviously mutual, but it is Unyŏng who first makes contact with Kim and who outlines a plan for their secret tryst at the palace. The description of their love is also less physical and more spiritual as the following account of their first union describes:

> I put out the lamp and went to the sleeping mat with him; the pleasure of that night I cannot describe with words. The night soon turned to dawn; as the rooster urged the daybreak, the *chinsa* rose and went back. From that time on, there was not a night that he did not come at dusk and take leave at dawn. Our love became deeper, and our affection for each other grew even warmer: we did not know how to stop these meetings.[55]

Far from a male-dominated relationship, the narrator tells of a mutually satisfactory physical relationship and a blooming love between the couple.

Kim Kyŏngmi examined the roles of men and women in early- to mid-Chosŏn fiction and has written that narratives such as *Chu saeng-jŏn* and *Wei Kyŏngch'ŏn-jŏn* demonstrate the hardships that the male protagonists must experience in order to consummate

---

[54] *Wei Kyŏngch'ŏn-jŏn*, 77.

[55] *Unyŏng-jŏn*, 45.

their love affairs.[56] It is thus the men who propel these affairs, and the hardships they experience are central to these works. Such a worldview in these novels reveals clear beliefs by the writers of the natural domination of sex and sexual needs by men, with women being simply the recipients of male desires. We do not see female sexual desire in these works, but rather women's submission to men.

Unyŏng-jŏn demonstrates a much different case as both the sexual and emotional longing of Unyŏng is the focus of the narrative. At the first meeting between Unyŏng and Kim, the reader feels the headlong rush into love of a young woman: "I was only a young woman at that time. When I looked at the *chinsa* once, I felt dizzy and my heart thumped. While the *chinsa* looked at me, he smiled and often eyed me carefully."[57] This description clearly reveals the mutual attraction between the two, yet the reader sees this blossoming relationship through the emotions of Unyŏng. This marks a significant departure from male-led romances of the period.

A contrasting scene of a first encounter is found in *Wei Kyŏngch'ŏn-jŏn* when the protagonist spies a woman of great beauty and sets his heart on bedding her: "Mr. Wei instantly realized that this [action] could cause his death, but his lust seethed beyond control."[58] Rather than an emotion like love, the above description demonstrates a baser carnality that must be satiated at any cost. The difference with the encounter in *Unyŏng-jŏn* is vivid and clearly juxtaposes love with libidinousness.

After the first meeting with Kim, Unyŏng seems completely infatuated. While some scholars see a more gradual process of falling in love, particularly that Unyŏng wanted to make certain of Kim's feelings for her,[59] the words of Unyŏng describing her emotional state after the first meeting seem to indicate her mind: "From that time on, although I lay down I could not sleep, my heart was so tormented that I could not eat any meals and did not know even if my clothes kept me warm."[60] Although this declaration was made in retrospect to her friend Charan, the fact that Unyŏng next wrote a poem to Kim announcing her feelings for

---

56 Kim Kyŏngmi, "*Unyŏng-jŏn*-e nat'anan yŏsŏng sŏsulja ŭi ŭiŭi," 49.

57 *Unyŏng-jŏn,* 16.

58 *Wei Kyŏngch'ŏn-jŏn,* 76.

59 Kim Kyŏngmi holds that Unyŏng verified Kim's feelings for her through a letter before fully falling in love. See Kim Kyŏngmi, "*Unyŏng-jŏn*-e nat'anan yŏsŏng sŏsulja ŭi ŭiŭi," 50–51.

60 *Unyŏng-jŏn,* 20.

him seems to verify that she had set her mind on him. Such a bold overture by Unyŏng also demonstrates the emotional strength of the character, as a woman approaching a man in such a manner would have been unheard of at the time. This is yet another marker of the uniqueness of the protagonist of *Unyŏng-jŏn.*

Unyŏng's insistence on realizing her wishes and her deep understanding of the social inequities that have confined her to a solitary life isolated in the royal palace demonstrate a sense of social righteousness far ahead of the times. In her first letter to Kim, Unyŏng reveals her life story and common background. Thus she is without the inherent sense of entitlement that those of the uppermost classes in the mid-Chosŏn period commonly possessed. She is keenly aware of the social limitations placed upon her as both a woman and a possession of the Grand Prince. Her anguish at this is seen in the letter she gives to Kim:

> Not being born a man, I could not rise in the world and gain fame, and as an unfortunate rose-cheeked woman, I was secluded in this deep palace for the ages. Owing to this, bitterness has bound my mind, and [my] deep resentment could fill the ocean. This past autumn night when I saw your face, I felt in my heart that you were a heavenly being who had descended to this world. I am not any less pretty than the other nine [palace women]; from what destiny of a previous life would the single drop from your writing brush cause the onset of this bitterness and sorrow in my heart? Looking at you through the beaded blinds, I imagined my fate as your wife, and seeing you in my dreams, I continued the love that I will never forget.[61]

The letter is telling for two points: Unyŏng's awareness and resentment of the Chosŏn social system, which excluded women from scholarship and government service, and her utter lack of the power to realize her heart's desire. This passage evinces a clear understanding of practices in Chosŏn that resulted in women being treated as inherently inferior to men. For the protagonist, the fundamental inequity is as simple as being born a woman. In her words, there is no possibility of a concept such as equality for a woman in Chosŏn society, regardless of her talent or intelligence. A woman is relegated automatically to an inferior position and a life of subservience to men.

---

[61] *Unyŏng-jŏn,* 38–39.

In addition, the life of the protagonist is further restricted by her isolation at the royal palace. Thus, she cannot find an outlet for either her creative capacities or her emotional and physical desires. Her deep sorrow and depression are the result of these two layers of bonds placed upon her. Her meeting with Kim sparks the awakening of her self-awareness at her plight and opens the floodgates of emotional desperation. With such a clear recognition of her miserable and marginal existence, Unyŏng cannot possibly return to her former life after feeling the surge of passion that the chance meeting with Kim brings about.

With her self-awakening, Unyŏng also rejects the possibility of a physical relationship with the Grand Prince. The relationship between Unyŏng and the Grand Prince is not overt, but the text is sprinkled with hints that Anp'yŏng wishes to take her as a lover, and such a situation is frequently acknowledged by her fellow palace women. Unyŏng nonetheless resists Anp'yŏng. Even shortly before taking her life, Unyŏng speaks fondly of Anp'yŏng, but this is the love a daughter might feel for her father, not a love of physical desire.[62]

The death of Unyŏng can therefore be argued as resulting from her self-awakening, not from the termination of her love affair with Kim. She decides to end their affair when the Grand Prince accuses her a second time of being unchaste. For fear of bringing ruin to all the women of the Western Palace, she tells Kim that they must no longer see each other and gives him a letter with her last wishes and her hopes that he will excel in his studies. Despite her strong love for Kim, Unyŏng realizes that continuing the affair will destroy many others.

Her suicide, then, is not a result of losing Kim, but rather her realization that life as a palace woman in the servitude of Anp'yŏng would be more than she is able or willing to endure. Having tasted love and experienced unbridled passion, Unyŏng understands that a return to the isolation of the royal palace and the emptiness of life therein is not bearable. While the impossibility of continuing her affair with Kim is a contributing factor, it is her unwillingness to again submit to the inhumane bonds of servitude that cause her to take her own life. She thus experiences an awakening to free choice, and the loss of this is the most salient factor in her death.

---

[62] Chŏng Ch'urhŏn, *Kojŏn sosŏlsa ŭi kudu wa sigak*, 115.

Kim *chinsa*

For all the strength and determination of the female protagonist in *Unyŏng-jŏn,* the male protagonist seems to embody the opposite traits. If Unyŏng can be said to be a strong woman, Kim seems to reflect a weak and oftentimes indecisive man. Unyŏng provides the initiative for the couple's union, while Kim seems unable to work out the simplest details without help from others. In fact, Kim's naïveté leads ultimately to Unyŏng's death. He is, in many ways, a mirror of a stereotypical Confucian scholar: erudite and deeply imbued with ethics, but unable to deal with those mundane elements outside his scholarly realm of limited knowledge.

The character of Kim is not fashioned as fully as that of Unyŏng; aside from his opening comments to Yu Yŏng, he is mostly seen through Unyŏng's eyes. Noteworthy in his first encounter with the Grand Prince is his depth of knowledge of literary tradition and his humility, the hallmarks of a Chosŏn-period man of high status. The narrative also reveals a degree of shyness in Kim, especially in the scenes where he seeks to have the shaman deliver a letter to Unyŏng. He seems almost afraid to speak his mind to this very aggressive woman.

Kim sees himself as a failure in terms of the societal expectations for a man of his status. Even before Unyŏng begins to tell her story to Yu Yŏng, Kim introduces himself as follows:

> At my young age and with a gallant nature, it was not easy to suppress my stalwart heart. Moreover, because of my fate with this woman, this body bequeathed by my parents became unfilial. What good in the world would it serve to know one sinner's name?[63]

His worldview is thus flavored heavily by the Confucian ethics in which he had long been immersed. The reader can see his disgust, at least at a level of morality, in the fact that he became involved in an affair that caused him to break the most sacred of the three bonds, that of filial piety.

Yet as the narrative unfolds, it is clear that Kim deeply loved, and continues to love, Unyŏng. He willingly entered into a relationship with her and affirmed his feelings for her in both his written and spoken words. His first letter to her well depicts the depth of his emotions:

[63] *Unyŏng-jŏn,* 5.

> From the time we bound our destiny with one look, my heart has grown restless, my spirit has gone out, and my mind cannot be easily pacified. Every time I look to the west of the palace,[64] it seems as if my bowels have been severed. With the letter that you passed me the other day through the wall, I humbly received your beautiful and unforgettable writing. Before I could unfold the whole letter, my breath was taken away, and before I finished half the letter, my tears had drenched the writing. From that time, I could not eat any food although I tried to eat. Illness has touched the deepest part of my chest and no sort of medicine will revive me. May heaven consider me pitiful and may ghosts help me silently. If ever, once in my life, my sorrow is relieved, I will purposely grind my body and make powder of my bones, and present rites to the myriad spirits in this world under heaven. While writing this letter, a lump binds my throat; what else can I say further?[65]

However, in retrospect, Kim seems to blame Unyŏng for their affair. For this reason, Kim Kyŏngmi argues that Unyŏng alone holds true love in this narrative as demonstrated by her unwavering love for Kim.[66] While I concur that Unyŏng is the character who does not sway from her love in this narrative, it is interesting to note that Kim is the one who gives up on life after Unyŏng's death, seemingly dying from a broken heart.

If Kim was somewhat overwhelmed in his relationship with Unyŏng, he was completely taken advantage of in his dealings with the slave T'ŭk. T'ŭk's cunningness is highly reminiscent of the slaves portrayed in masked-dance dramas, who outwit their upper-class masters.[67] Yet T'ŭk is not portrayed in quite the same light as the clever slaves in folk dramas, as he lacks any sort of redeeming quality whatsoever. Motivated entirely by greed and gut-level salacious emotions, the character of T'ŭk embodies a fearful and evil presence in the narrative. While Unyŏng soon recognizes T'ŭk's deceits, Kim gullibly supports the slave until his treacherous deceit lands squarely upon Kim and the repeated betrayals become vividly apparent.

---

64 That is, the location of Susŏng Palace.

65 *Unyŏng-jŏn*, 25.

66 Kim Kyŏngmi, "*Unyŏng-jŏn*-e nat'anan yŏsŏng sŏsulja ŭi ŭiŭi," 58–59.

67 Interestingly, some accounts of mid-Chosŏn life seem to demonstrate that masters oftentimes had little control over the actions of their slaves. Theft, flight, and insubordination appear to have been commonplace. See Kichung Kim, "Unheard Voices: The Life of the Nobi in O Hwi-mun's *Swaemirok*."

The relationship between these two men seems, at least superficially, to be a rather typical one of a naïve scholar and resourceful slave. Examining this from the perspective of the writer of this narrative seems to reveal both a distrust and a fear of slaves. The fact that the lower-class slave continually outsmarts a *yangban* male perhaps hints that the writer of this narrative was not of the uppermost status group. The presence of physical fear also indicates that the writer was not in a position to easily subdue a renegade slave by either legal measures or physical force. While the sense of loathing for such a despicable human is clear in the narrative, there is also an equally strong sense of helplessness in the face of such a danger.

The portrayal of T'ŭk might suggest an answer to the authorship of *Unyŏng-jŏn*. An upper-status male writer would hardly have been in awe of a slave and, moreover, would have been loath to create a narrative in which the slave continually manipulates his master to the degree found in *Unyŏng-jŏn*. The writer of this novel was an individual who would not have been able to easily fend off the assault of a corrupt slave, someone who would not have had the full support of the legal system or the economic wherewithal to ensure a dominant relationship. The writer might have also desired to create a satirical portrayal showing the incompetence of the *yangban* scholars, who were at the apex of Chosŏn society.

As inept as Kim might have been in his dealings with his slave, he equally excelled in building a close relationship with Anp'yŏng. From the first meeting of the two, a truly close bond was formed. Their closeness was not that of royal master and minister, however. Rather, the bond between the two was closer to that of an elder brother to a younger brother. The comfort level that Anp'yŏng felt toward Kim resulted in his allowing the palace women to remain in the presence of the visitor. This oversight, of course, begins the relationship between Kim and Unyŏng.

A subtle hint to Kim's passionate outlook on life is revealed in his debate with Anp'yŏng on the Chinese master poets. Kim criticizes the poetry of the Tang master Du Fu (712–770) as follows: "If we only talk about what the ordinary Confucians venerate, that is same as saying raw meat and roasted meat are pleasing to the people's mouths. Zimei's poems are deliberately raw meat and roasted meat."[68] Kim finds the poetry of Du Fu to be too

---

[68] *Unyŏng-jŏn*, 18. Zimei is the courtesy name of Du Fu.

ordinary and not passionate enough to adequately describe human emotions. Interestingly, while Anp'yŏng acknowledges the correctness of Kim's observation, he does not view the young scholar as a "man" and thus does not notice the spark between him and Unyŏng.

The delicate nature of Kim's character is seen at several points in the narrative, but perhaps nowhere as vividly as when he awaits Unyŏng at the shaman's house. He does not impatiently wait or drink to pass the time while waiting for her. Rather, he sits in the corner, wrings his hands and sobs. Such a countenance is unlike any other we see for a male character in Chosŏn fiction: this does not seem a man's description of how men act, but rather, perhaps, a woman's vision of a man in love. Likewise, Kim's bumbling incompetence in sneaking into the palace is not how a male protagonist is commonly portrayed. It is the very weakness of Kim's character, however, that brings the strength of Unyŏng to the fore.

Even Kim's actions at the end of the narrative demonstrate his weakness relative to Unyŏng. As mentioned above, Unyŏng takes her own life proactively rather than face a lifetime of confinement and solitude at the palace. Kim, on the other hand, struggles to carry out her wishes after her death. In fact, he does not personally go to the temple to make offerings on behalf of Unyŏng, but again employs the guileful T'ŭk for this task. And again, the slave deceives his gullible master. After finally offering prayers on behalf of Unyŏng, Kim then dies—but unlike Unyŏng, who chases death by hanging herself, Kim dies a passive death, lying and waiting four days for death to come to him. Such an end to these two lives amply demonstrates the inherent strengths and weaknesses of these characters.

Considering the weakness of Kim's character vis-à-vis Unyŏng's from the perspective of the writer, it could be posited that the character of Kim was intentionally made weak to highlight the strength of Unyŏng. What end would such a contrast serve? Perhaps it was meant to bring into relief that women are as capable as men and to illustrate the unfairness of a Confucian social system that systematically categorized women as inherently subordinate to men.

The Writer's Voice

As in any fictional prose, the voice of the writer can be found throughout the text in the voices and actions of the characters. In

Unyŏng-jŏn the primary carrier of the writer's opinions is the protagonist, Unyŏng. Her innermost thoughts and aspirations might also reflect those of the writer as too could her critique of social systems and ethics.

What could the writer have wished to convey to readers? The inherent message in *Unyŏng-jŏn* is, I think, the desire for autonomy concerning freedom of choice. The text has numerous points where practices such as bringing young women to the palace to live in perpetual servitude to the royals, disallowing freedom of choice in love relations, and denying the opportunity to choose one's life path are vividly brought into question. Through the plight of Unyŏng, inhumane practices denying basic freedoms are depicted lucidly. The debates and conversations among the palace women bring into even sharper focus what is being denied to the women in this narrative. At one point in the narrative, Charan asks her comrades, "'What sin have the ten of us alone committed that we must be fettered to this isolated and lonely palace, while the spring flowers and autumn moon pass? Always oppressed by false rules: why are we destined to such a cruel fate?'"[69]

Possibly we can understand the writer's intent through this short passage, and this is to bring into question the right of one group of humans to dominate and subjugate another. The "false rules" that permitted the ruling elites to oppress the palace women seem the target of the writer's criticism.

[69] *Unyŏng-jŏn*, 30.

CHAPTER FOUR

Chosŏn Society as Revealed in *Unyŏng-jŏn*

Important considerations concerning *Unyŏng-jŏn* include how readers of the mid- to late-Chosŏn period engaged this narrative and what that engagement reveals about life in the Chosŏn dynasty. The narrative reflects many aspects of life in early-seventeenth-century Korea, some obvious to the twenty-first century reader and others buried under thick layers of changed circumstances and worldviews. This analysis is not meant to be exclusive or exhaustive inasmuch as the dynamic relationship between readers and the text would have permitted myriad understandings and reactions. What this investigation seeks is to provide a foundation for appraising the value of this text to readers, particularly women, in the late-Chosŏn period.

As with any literary work, a reader's engagement with *Unyŏng-jŏn* would have varied depending upon a host of factors including gender, social status, time period, and personal life experiences. The reaction of a palace woman reader and that of an upper-class male *yangban* reader would have been greatly different. So too would have been the reaction among those of different life experiences. A woman in a happy marriage might not have felt strong empathy for the plight of Unyŏng, whereas a woman in a less than ideal marriage might have felt a deep bond with the protagonist and her hardships. Accordingly, we can only make general inferences based upon certain assumptions concerning the demographics of the readers of this work.

Determining the readership of this work is an excellent starting point for this analysis, and an important and interesting consideration. As this work was initially written in literary Chinese, we can assume that most early readers would have been men, save for the few women possessing sufficient education to manage such a lengthy and difficult work. Such a group of well-educated women included some members of the royal family, women of high status, and palace women. The fact that a woman could not read literary Chinese, however, would not exclude her from sharing in this work. While professional novel readers (*iyagi-kkun*) who earned money reading novels to groups of people cannot be verified until the eighteenth century, the practice of informally reading a novel or other written work to family members or others is undoubtedly as old as the use of writing systems in Korea. Accordingly, literacy was not prerequisite to enjoying a work such as *Unyŏng-jŏn*.

Within a few decades of the creation of *Unyŏng-jŏn*, at most, the novel was translated into hangul, allowing a much broader readership not limited by knowledge of literary Chinese. And there seems little doubt among most scholars that the largest readership of hangul novels was most assuredly women of middle- to upper-status families.[1] The popularity of *Unyŏng-jŏn* is verified in the numerous editions created over the last half of the Chosŏn period.

A consequence of the tremendous popularity of novels among women led to an explosion in the number of book-lending shops (*sech'aekka*) in Hanyang and also in the number of traveling peddlers who lent books along with selling various household sundries.[2] The number of these shops and of the novels available for readers was impressive, with one early-twentieth-century commentator citing a single shop with more than 120 titles and 3,200 total books.[3] While reports are most likely exaggerated to some degree, men saw the influence of novels as being ruinous for women. The following note was written by Ch'ae Chegong (1720–1779), who served as second state councilor (*chwaŭijŏng*):

> All that womenfolk of these days are eager to do is to read novels. As days and months pass, the number [of novels] has reached to more than eleven hundred types. Brokers cleanly copy [the novels] and earn money by receiving payment each time they lend the books. Since womenfolk are not knowledgeable, they sell their

---

[1] See Kim Yŏnsuk, *Kososŏl ŭi yŏsŏng chuŭijŏk yŏn'gu*, 12–13; Chŏng Haeŭn, "Ponggŏn ch'eje ŭi tongyo wa yŏsŏng ŭi sŏngjang," 229–233; O Chonggŭn and Paek Miae, *Chosŏnjo kajŏng sosŏl yŏn'gu*, 126–128.

[2] Chŏng Haeŭn, "Ponggŏn ch'eje ŭi tongyo wa yŏsŏng ŭi sŏngjang," 232. For book lending in general, see Yi Yunsŏk, Otani Morishige, and Chŏng Myŏnggi, eds., *Sech'aek kososŏl yŏn'gu*.

[3] The commentator was Ch'oe Namsŏn. See Chŏng Ch'anggwŏn, *Han'guk kojŏn yŏsŏng sosŏl ŭi chaebalgyŏn*, 61–62.

> hairpins and bracelets, or go into debt, to borrow the books that allow them to spend their long days, sometimes forgetting to eat or sleep.[4]

This commentary was written in the preface of his wife's copy of *Yŏsasŏ* [The four books for women], perhaps has a reminder of the baneful influence of fictional works such as novels.

As similar accounts to the one above are common, we must consider why novels were thought to be negative influences on the people in general and women specifically. Of course, the disdain that the Confucian elite in general held for fiction is a factor. The following passage concerning novels is included in part of a late-eighteenth-century didactic work for upper-status families:

> Popular romances and novels teach guileful and licentious behaviors and thus should not be read. One should forbid children to read these works. Sometimes one might meet a person who speaks at length about these books, even urging to read them. How pitiful. How can one's ignorance reach such a depth?[5]

Novels allowed people to see alternative behaviors and oftentimes did not support mores such as loyalty and hierarchy essential for the maintenance of Chosŏn society. This was particularly true for women, it seems, as the following account from the same text demonstrates:

> Women should not indulge in *ŏnmun* [i.e., hangul] novels and neglect household duties and women's chores. Further, there are those who squander the family's fortune by borrowing these books from lending libraries. The content [of these novels] is all about jealousy and lewd activities and not infrequently these works cause women to plunge into licentiousness.[6]

Yet by late Chosŏn, men who composed fiction for "proper" reasons were not censored, but even praised. Such is the case with Kim Manjung (1637–1692), who composed both *Kuun-mong* [A dream of nine clouds] and *Sassi namjŏnggi* [A record of lady Sa's trip to the south]; the former work is said to have been written to relieve his mother of her worries after his exile, and the other created as an act of loyalty to admonish King Sukchong (r. 1674–1720). Although the genre of the novel was not highly

---

[4] Quoted in Chŏng Haeŭn, "Ponggŏn ch'eje ŭi tongyo wa yŏsŏng ŭi sŏngjang," 231–232.

[5] Yi Tŏkmu, *Sasojŏl*, 107.

[6] Ibid., 272.

valued by elites, its value as a medium for conveying Confucian morality was recognized.

Women, however, found other qualities in novels that fanned their interest. In particular, novels permitted momentary escape from otherwise sometimes oppressive lives and empowerment through fictional characters. Women readers could vicariously experience situations that reality would never afford them such as leading troops in battle as seen in *Pakssi-jŏn* [The tale of Lady Pak], life and love at the royal palace as told in *Unyŏng-jŏn,* and the overcoming of social barriers and finding true love as depicted in *Sukhyang-jŏn* [The tale of Sukhyang].[7] Such positive characters further allowed an encounter with another woman's voice and life.

Foremost to understanding *Unyŏng-jŏn* is comprehension of how the novel form challenged notions supported by the existing literary tradition in Chosŏn. Not unlike the advent of the novel in Europe, the appearance of the novel in Korea caused repercussions in other literary forms. Mikhail Bakhtin wrote that the novel "gets on poorly with other genres. It fights for its own hegemony in literature; wherever it triumphs, the other older genres go into decline."[8] In Chosŏn, where literature was understood as a tool for cultivating morality, this is perhaps all the more true.

In Chosŏn, the novel introduced such new ideas as realism, idealism, romanticism, and fantasy.[9] Although all these notions had previously circulated to some degree in orally transmitted narratives, the development of the novel genre allowed both more regular transmissions and broader audiences. The novel also carried numerous themes that challenged the orthodox worldview of the Chosŏn elites, particularly in regard to ideas concerning class structure and social role. For example, *Hong Kiltong-jŏn* [The tale of Hong Kiltong] holds a discourse highly critical of discrimination against sons of secondary wives or concubines, and *Kuunmong* is founded in a decidedly Buddhist worldview that dismisses secular Confucianism and instead promotes the value of a transcendent life of rejecting worldly fame.[10] Novels provided

---

[7] *Pakssi-jŏn* is an anonymous work that tells of a woman general during the Manchu invasion of 1636, while *Sukhyang-jŏn* tells of a woman who undergoes great hardships but is still able to realize her love for a man of a higher class.

[8] Mikhail Bakhtin, *The Dialogic Imagination,* 4.

[9] Chŏng Ch'urhŏn, *Kojŏn sosŏlsa ŭi kudu wa sigak,* 57–65.

[10] *Hong Kiltong-jŏn* is commonly attributed to Hŏ Kyun (1569–1618), although most scholars agree that the presently extant version of this work was probably written later.

an excellent stage for alternative and heterodox visions of society.

Unyŏng-jŏn represents such a subversive tradition. The work clearly demonstrates the inequities of the Chosŏn social system, particularly in regard to basic human freedoms such as the pursuit of love and self-fulfillment. Unyŏng's forced entry into servitude at the royal palace displays the fundamental unjustness of a society that allowed certain classes to enslave others. The female voice of the work also provided women readers reassurance and validation: reassurance that their own emotions and frustrations were shared by others and validation of their own self-worth as humans. Thereby, despite the physical isolation enforced upon women of upper-status groups, a work such as *Unyŏng-jŏn* allowed a sense of community. Pam Morris writes that this is a hallmark of works by women writers as it allows the encounter with another woman's voice through which female readers can hear the sound of their own voice.[11]

We see subversiveness at other points in the novel. Unyŏng, while always respectful of Anp'yŏng and his wife, longs for her natal family. Her comfort and cherished memories are there, not in service at the royal palace. She also finds her greatest solace in the companionship of her fellow palace women, reinforcing the bond of female comradeship. Both of these factors demonstrate the writer's awareness in the importance of relationships mostly disallowed to upper-status women in Chosŏn. Relations with the natal family were largely cut off after marriage for most women, and numerous female friends, especially those outside one's husband's family, were difficult to foster because of the lack of freedom. The conclusion of this novel also disavows the restraints put upon the lives of women as Unyŏng takes her own life rather than conform to life in thrall of a repressive social system.

The literary forms found in *Unyŏng-jŏn* allowed for a more accurate portrayal of emotions. Especially, changes in literary styles in the seventeenth century permitted this novel to carry deeply emotional contents. The prominence of Tang-style poetry in *Unyŏng-jŏn* is reflective of larger literary trends of the middle-Chosŏn period. Tang poetry came into vogue during the late sixteenth century and replaced the heretofore dominant Song-style poetry known as the Haedong kangsŏ (Eastern Jiangxi) school of poetry. The Haedong kangsŏ poets were highly restricted by emphasis on intricate rhetorical devices and allusions to obscure

[11] Pam Morris, *Literature and Feminism*, 64.

historical precedents; moreover, a great importance was placed on the role of poetry and cultivating the way of Confucianism. Poetry was understood as a means to create a bond with nature, the ideal space for understanding the Confucian principles of the universe and avoiding the vulgar world and its temptations. Among these shunned temptations were base human emotions such as desire and sexual love.

Tang poetry, on the other hand, is imbued with the emotions and experiences of everyday life. By appealing to basic human emotions such as love, it allowed expression of sentiments long suppressed by the Song-style poets. This exploration of basic human desires such as love results in the skepticism of the Confucian social system manifested in *Unyŏng-jŏn*. Chŏng Hwan'guk has argued that this skepticism in *Unyŏng-jŏn* is a result of the flourishing of Tang-style poetry affirming basic human nature and desires and the Wang Yang-ming philosophy that also supported human emotions.[12] The literary forms in *Unyŏng-jŏn* reflect the changes that society was experiencing in the tumultuous period after the Japanese invasions (1592–1598) and around the Manchu invasions (1627, 1636).

It is clear that *Unyŏng-jŏn* must have been a very popular work given the numerous versions extant. The worldview of the novel and the questions that it raises concerning the early-seventeenth-century social system would have been provocative for women readers of the day. Women, who in reality could not have fully rebelled against the value system of Chosŏn that restricted their lives, would have found in this work an alternative understanding of life, self-worth, and empowerment.

The model established with Unyŏng also provided women a proxy through which they could vicariously experience the emotional zeniths found in love, passion, and autonomy. The voice carried in this novel would have spoken clearly to those readers who had an absence of such experiences in their own lives, on one hand, and reaffirmed the importance of these traits to others in more favorable circumstances. The life of Unyŏng, while far from ideal in many aspects, could have given women readers a means to come to terms with their own lot, and the cathartic release from the emotional peaks and valleys experienced by Unyŏng would have permitted women to contend with everyday drudgery caused

---

[12] Chŏng Hwan'guk, "16 segi mal 17 segi ch'o sasangsa ŭi hŭrŭm sok esŏ pŏn *Unyŏng-jŏn*," 261–292.

by highly restricted personal freedoms. Certainly not every reader would have bonded with the protagonist, but many women must have felt a tremendous empathy with the plight of Unyŏng. Such mental relief and bonding would have provided the psychological strength to continue their own lives.

This was the great value of *Unyŏng-jŏn* to women readers of the last half of the Chosŏn dynasty. The work would have reaffirmed the value of their lives and their self-worth. Such a strong voice as that of the female protagonist would have spoken loudly to readers and awakened a sense of individual agency opposed to the social system that devalued women and their importance as humans. While readers certainly did not rise up in open rebellion against such a repressive social system, we can envision that women readers would have experienced a surge of empowerment and carried this forth in their own lives, perhaps seeking to find a space for personal agency and control.

CHAPTER FIVE

Unyŏng-jŏn: Translation

Susŏng Palace, the old residence of Grand Prince Anp'yŏng, was situated to the west of Changan Castle at the foot of the Inwang Mountains.[1] The mountains and streams were so graceful that it seemed a dragon would soon appear, and also were so steep and rugged that they appeared like a crouched tiger. To the south was Sajik and the east, Kyŏngbok Palace.[2]

The Inwang Mountains meandered up and down, forming a high peak near the spot of Susŏng Palace. Although not high, if one went to the top and looked down, the shops scattered along the road and the houses in the capital looked like a *paduk* board[3] and also—like stars in the heavens—one could clearly see the details. The shape was as ordered as a loom clearly separates thread. If one looked to the east, the palace was in the distance and the double road to it seemed suspended in the air.[4] The

---

[1] Grand Prince Anp'yŏng (1418–1453) was the third son of King Sejong (r. 1418–1450). His given name was Yong, his courtesy name Ch'ŏngji, and pen names Pihaedang and Maejukhŏn. His residence was Susŏng-gung Palace.

Changan Castle is actually the royal city of Tang China (618–907). In this instance, it refers to Kyŏngbok Palace.

Inwang-san is within the old city walls of Seoul. The elevation of the main peak is 338 meters.

[2] Sajik Altar was founded in 1394 by King T'aejo (r. 1392–1398). The kings of Chosŏn would perform rites to the deities of the earth (*t'osin*) and grains (*koksin*) on behalf of the people at this altar.

Kyŏngbok-kung was built under orders from King T'aejo in 1394 and destroyed by rampaging slaves during the Hideyoshi Invasion in 1592. The palace was in ruins for nearly three centuries before being rebuilt near the end of the Chosŏn dynasty in 1872.

[3] *Paduk* is a board game played on a board crossed with horizontal and vertical lines.

[4] The double road (*pokto*) refers to the roads leading to the royal palace. The upper road was reserved for use by the king, and the lower road for others.

clouds and smoke were bluer in the morning and evening, intensifying its elegance all the more; it was truly peerless in beauty.

Drinking parties, groups of archers, poets and artists, or singing boys and flute-playing boys—at the time of the blossoming flowers in the third month or the changing foliage in the ninth month, surely there was not a day when such a group would not go up for pleasure.[5] While enjoying a clear breeze or brightly shining moon, they would almost forget to return home.

Yu Yŏng, a literatus of Ch'ŏngpa, had grown used to hearing of this peak's beautiful scenery.[6] He sincerely wished to go there and enjoy it as well. However, with shabby clothes and a gaunt face he knew he would only be ridiculed by the pleasure-seekers [on the mountain peak]. For long, he hesitated about going there.

In spring, on the sixteenth day of the third month of 1601,[7] he bought a jug of wine, fastened the liquor bottle on his person, and walked out. Alone, he entered the western castle gate. When the other sightseers looked at him, there was not a single occasion that they did not point and laugh. Scholar Yu was ashamed and, feeling bad, he quickly went out to the rear garden. He went up to a high point, looked out over the four quarters, and saw the remains of the fires of the recent war.[8] Looking over the site of Changan Palace,[9] he saw no trace of the palace or the gorgeous houses inside the castle walls. Among the fallen walls, shattered roof tiles, buried wells, and the stone steps turned to clods of earth was only a dense growth of trees and grass.

Scholar Yu entered the Western Garden, deep in a remote mountain area. There were thick growths of every kind of grass, casting shadows upon a clear pond. The ground was covered with fallen flower petals and had not yet been touched by human footprints. With every stir of the breeze, one's nose was pierced with fragrance.

---

5 Singing boys (*kaa*) and flute-playing boys (*chŏktong*) commonly accompanied upper-class men on their outings.

6 Ch'ŏngpa was a district in the capital of Hansŏng. This area is presently in Yongsan-gu.

7 The text notes that this happened on *manryŏk sinch'uk samwŏl kimang*. *Manryŏk* was the reign title for Emperor Shenzong (r. 1573–1619) of Ming China (1368–1644). *Sinch'ŭk* year indicates the twenty-ninth year of his reign, or 1601. *Samwŏl* is the third lunar month. The sixteenth day of each month is *kimang* according to the traditional method for reckoning dates.

8 The war referred to here is the Hideyoshi invasions of 1592–1598.

9 Again, this refers to Kyŏngbok Palace.

Scholar Yu sat on a rock, reciting, "When I came up to Chowŏn Hall, although spring had already ripened, there was none to sweep the abundant fallen flowers," a line from a poem written by Su Dongpo.[10] Soon after, he untied the liquor bottle he was carrying and drank it all down, and then drunkenly lay back, using a stone near the rock as a pillow.

Shortly, when he sobered up and turned to look around, the pleasure seekers had all scattered and were gone. The moon rose above the hill while smoke warmly enveloped the willow branches and wind caressed the flower petals. Suddenly, a strand of soft words rode in on the breeze. Yu, thinking it strange, rose and moved toward it. Sitting face to face were a youth and an unparalleled beauty. Seeing Yu, they joyfully greeted him. Yu looked at the young man and asked him, "Young sir, what kind of person are you to linger about with this beauty at night?"

The young man grinned. "What the people of olden times called stopping in the middle of the road to talk is exactly what happened in our case."[11]

Thus, the three sat in a triangle and began to talk. In a somewhat soft voice, the beauty summoned servants, and out of the woods appeared two maidservants. She spoke to them. "In this place where I have fortuitously met my old love, I also unexpectedly met a delightful guest. Consequently, tonight will not be passed in lonely futility. Prepare a table of savory food and drink for us."

The two maidservants received the order and left; shortly, they returned with a table to serve the three. Each took turns in offering a cup of liquor to the others. As for the taste of the liquor and food, it was all not of the human world. Warmed by the wine, the woman sang a new verse:

In the deep and vast palace, I separated with my love of yore,
The affinity of heaven is not so harsh, [thus] I met him again.
Becoming clouds, becoming rain: the pleasure was
merely a dream.[12]

---

[10] Su Dongpo refers to Su Shi (1036–1101), a poet of the Northern Sung dynasty (960–1127) whose pen name was Dongpo. Chowŏn Hall was a Daoist shrine in Tang China where rites to Laozi were performed. The poem mentioned here is "Lishan" [Mount black horse] and is in *Dongpo quanji* [The collected works of Dongpo], vol. 28.

[11] The text reads *kyŏnggae yakku,* which indicates a friendly relationship to the extent of stopping in the road to chat. Here, it implies a very close relationship from long ago between the young man and woman.

[12] The line "becoming clouds, becoming rain" refers to a tale of the Chinese

How deep have I been tormented on spring days
of blooming flowers?
All of this has vanished and become a mote,
Yet it still makes me drench my handkerchief with vain tears.

After finishing the song, she sighed heavily and sobbed, with gemstone-like tears covering her face. Yu, thinking this odd, asked, "Even if I have no talent for composing refined, silk-like verse, from early on I was devoted to letters and ink[13] and know something of the merits of literature. Now, I have heard your song, which is exceedingly sonorous and excellent. However, the poetic sentiment is very sorrowful and makes me curious. Tonight, opportunely, the moonlight illuminates like daytime, and a cool breeze gently blows; despite such a lovely night worth enjoying why do you sit facing each other and cry? Also, as you do not tell me your names or speak of what is deep in your minds although the liquor has added to the fullness of the emotions, all I can do is wonder."

Yu gave his own name first and asked them to do the same. The youth sighed, answering, "There is a reason that I did not speak of my name, but as you insist on knowing it, why would it be difficult to tell you? However, it is a long story."

Looking sorrowful, he was silent for quite a while, and then spoke.

"My surname is Kim. When ten I could write poetry well and was famous at my village school. At fourteen I passed the primary state examination, and from that time everyone called me Kim *chinsa*. At my young age and with a gallant nature, it was not easy to suppress my stalwart heart. Moreover, because of my fate with this woman, this body bequeathed by my parents became unfilial. What good in the world would it serve to know one sinner's name? This woman is named Unyŏng, and the two maid-servants are Nokchu and Songok. They all were the palace women of Grand Prince Anp'yŏng of olden times."

Yu replied, "If you bring up the story and do not tell all, it is worse than not saying anything from the beginning. Tales of the

---

Ch'u kingdom (The pleasure of clouds and rain). King Xiang of Ch'u (?–223 BCE) took a nap one afternoon, a woman appeared in his dream, and they slept together. Later, the woman informed him that she lived on a high crag of Mt. Mu (C. Wushan; K. Musan) and that every morning she became a cloud and in the evening, rain. Consequently, the expression "becoming clouds, becoming rain" is a metaphor for sexual intercourse.

[13] That is, literature (*munmuk*).

time of Grand Prince Anp'yŏng and the reasons for the sorrow of a *chinsa*—can you tell me of these things in detail?"

The *chinsa* turned and looked at Unyŏng, saying, "Many seasons have passed and those days are already long past. Can you still recollect the events of those times?"

Unyŏng replied, "Bitterness fills my heart; on what day can I forget? While I will try to tell the story, my dearest, will you stay by my side and add to it when needed?"

Grasping a writing brush, and having her maidservant prepare an inkstone, she began her story.

King Sejong had eight grand princes, and among them, Grand Prince Anp'yŏng was the most sagacious.[14] The king loved him deeply and awarded him countless tax fields[15] and other commodities, more than any of the other grand princes. At thirteen he moved to a private palace named Susŏng. The Grand Prince considered that as a scholar he should study the Confucian Classics at night and compose poems or practice calligraphy during the day. Not for a moment did he stop studying. All the talented literary men of that time gathered at the palace and tested themselves against the Grand Prince. Truly, the discourse did not stop. Also, as for the Grand Prince's calligraphy, there were none who surpassed his talent.

One day the Grand Prince said to us palace women, "All of the talented men of this world must move to a tranquil place, and only after they study in such a locale are they able to achieve success. Since outside the eastern gate of the capital the mountains and streams are quiet and villages are distant, if one is to polish his knowledge there he can achieve great success."

Soon he had constructed a building of some ten rooms at that place. To one side he erected an altar named Pihae-dang and to the other side a shrine called Maengsi-dan.[16] It must have been his intention to lead people to think of righteousness through those names. All the men of letters and great calligraphers of the day gathered there. Sŏng Sammun was at the fore of the literary men, and Ch'oe Hŭnghyo was the best among the calligraphers.[17]

---

[14] The text uses an alternate title for the king, Changhŏn taewang. Sejong was the fourth king of Chosŏn and reigned from 1418 to 1450.

[15] *Chŏnmin.* This includes both fields, dry and paddy, and slaves.

[16] Pihae-dang can be translated as the Altar of No-Idleness, and Maengsi-dan as the Shrine of a Pledge to Poetry. It is further notable that Pihaedang is also one of the pen names of the Grand Prince.

[17] Sŏng Sammun (1418–1456) was a scholar-official at the Chiphyŏn-jŏn (Hall of

Nonetheless, they could not reach the level of the Grand Prince.

One evening the Grand Prince called [all of] us palace women together and said, "Talent comes down from the heavens, so why would men have abundance and women so little? Nowadays there are many in the world claiming to be men of letters, but among them, none stands out. From now on, you all should also study diligently!"

From among his palace women, he selected ten who were young of age and had beautiful faces, and began to teach us. First he taught us *Sohak ŏnhae* [Elementary learning with Korean annotations][18] and after we could recite that without help, he continued, teaching *Shiji* [Records of the historian] and all of the Classics; there was nothing we did not learn. We learned several hundred pieces of Tang verse such as those by Li Bai and Du Fu.[19] He would have us recite these morning and evening, and the discussion would not cease. As a result, within five years, all of us had reached a great level of talent.

When the Grand Prince returned from outside the palace, he would have us sit in front of him and then he would rank our poems from high to low, encouraging us through reward and punishment. Even though our excellent spirit could not approach the level of the Grand Prince, the elegance of our rhymes and perfect versification were worthy of peeking into the hedge surrounding the Tang poets of the golden age.[20] The names of us ten were Puyong, Piyŏng, Pich'wi, Ongnyŏ, Kŭmnyŏn, Ŭnsŏm, Charan, Poryŏn, Sook, and Unyŏng. Unyŏng is none other than me. The

---

Worthies) during King Sejong's reign. He is one of the scholars who helped in the creation of the hangul script during that time. Later, he refused to acknowledge the usurpation of the throne by Sejo (r. 1455–1468) and was executed, becoming known as one of the six martyred ministers (*sayuksin*). Ch'oe Hŭnghyo was also a civil official under the reign of Sejong, serving as second deputy director (*chikchehak*) in the Office of Royal Decrees (Yemun-gwan) beginning in 1421. Ch'oe and Grand Prince Anp'yŏng are acclaimed as being the best calligraphers of the age.

[18] This seems a factual error by the writer as *Sohak ŏnhae* was not first compiled until the reign of Chungjong (1506–1544), long after the death of Anp'yŏng.

[19] Tang verse refers to the poetry of the Tang dynasty (618–907). Li Bai (701–762) and Du Fu (712–770) were famous poets of Tang China.

[20] The poetry of the Tang dynasty is generally divided into four periods based on style, and Cheng-tang is the second of these periods, covering the time from the reign of Xuanzong (705–709) to Daizong (763–779). The other three periods are the early (Chu-tang), middle (Zhong-tang), and late (Man-tang). The Cheng-tang period is appraised as the zenith of poetic skill in Tang and was the age of renowned poets such as Li Bai and Du Fu.

Grand Prince cared for all of us greatly and always had us stay within the palace compound, not allowing us to even have a conversation with those from outside the palace. Every day the Grand Prince would drink with the literati who gathered to debate about poetry and such subjects, but not once did he permit us to come near the area, for he feared that the outsiders would possibly become aware of our existence. And there was always the command, "If anyone of you goes outside of the palace gate one time, for that crime she will suffer death. If an outsider knows one of your names, for that crime too you will not escape from death."

One day the Grand Prince came back from outside the palace and called us together saying, "Today I was drinking with the scholars so-and-so and there appeared a strand of blue smoke rising from trees within the palace compound. Some surrounded the top of the castle and some hovered at the foot of the mountains. First, I composed a poem and asked my guests to follow with their verses next.[21] However, not one was pleasing to me. Each of you write and offer up a verse in the order of your age."

Sook offered her verse first:

The blue smoke is slender as silk,
It follows the wind and comes in the palace gate.
It grows thick and again becomes thin,
I did not even notice dusk drawing near.

Then, each of the remaining nine gave their verses, beginning with Puyong:

It flies up to the heavens and brings rain,
Dropping to the earth and again becoming a cloud.
Evening falls and the mountain colors darken,
My deepest thought is yearning for the lord of Zhou.[22]

Pich'wi followed:

Clouds cover the flowers, bees lose their vigor,
Mottled in the bamboo grove, birds cannot find their roost.
At dusk misty drizzle falls,
Outside my window, I hear the sound of raindrops.

---

[21] A pentasyllabic quatrain.

[22] This line of the poem refers to the aforementioned legend of the pleasure of clouds and rain and the lover who takes the form of the clouds in the morning and the rain in the evening.

Then Pigyŏng:

While a small apricot tree struggles to even bud,
A solitary bamboo stands, never losing its green hue.
The light shade looks heavy in an instant,
The sun sinks and the dusk turns dark.

Next was Ognyŏ:

The sun-concealing cloud is light as silken gauze,
Traversing the mountains the verdant sash lies long.
By a gentle breeze it was slowly dissipated and,
Remaining is only enough to dampen a small lotus pond.

Then Kŭmnyŏn:

Below the mountain is filled with cold smoke,
It flows aslant by the palace trees.
In the blowing wind it scatters thither and fro,
Evening sunlight fills the blue heavens.

Next was Ŭnsŏm:

In the mountain ravine billowing clouds rise,
At the pavilion near the pond flows a green shadow.
It flies but cannot find the place to return,
Becoming dewdrop beads, it remains on the lotus leaf.

Charan followed:

In the early morning even the village entry[23] is dark,
The clouds lie obliquely and the tall trees appear low.
In a brief second, suddenly it flies off,
To the western mountain peak and the brook at its front.

I gave my verse next:

In the distant place,[24] the bluish smoke is a wisp,
The beauty stops weaving silken gauze.[25]

---

[23] This refers to the gate to a particular section of the city.

[24] The Asami version refers to a "water kingdom" (*suguk*) while the Changsŏgak version mentions a distant place (*wŏnmang*). "Water kingdom" seems to allude to a place that is distant and not easily attainable, and thus might be a more literary metaphor to a very distant or mythical place.

[25] The beauty weaving silk might be an allusion to Chignyŏ, the woman in the legend of the Weaver Girl and Shepherd Boy [*Kyŏnu-Chingyŏ sŏlhwa*]. This legend dates to the Chinese Zhou dynasty (1027 BCE–771 BCE) and tells the story of the daughter of the Jade Emperor and a shepherd who lived across the Milky Way. The two met and fell in love, and from that point forward both neglected their duties. The Jade Emperor thus forbade them to see one another. However, he felt pity for the two and allowed them to meet one day a year, the seventh day of the

In the wind, alone, disillusioned and sad,
It [the clouds] flies off and falls on Mt. Mu [becoming rain].[26]

Lastly, Poryŏn gave her verse:

From the dense shade of the small ravine,
From the misty breath of the capital it rises.[27]
Now, suddenly it turns the human world
Into a blue-jade beaded palace.

When the Grand Prince finished reading, he was greatly surprised. "Compared to the poems of the late Tang it is difficult to determine which is superior, and those not up to the level of Kŭnbo would not even be able to grasp the whip [for understanding these poems]."[28]

He then recited the poems two and three times again, still unable to appraise the relative merits of the poems. After a spell, he continued, "Puyong's poetic notion is longing for the lord of Zhou and thus I highly commend her for this. The rhyme and flow of Pich'wi's poem are beautiful,[29] and I consider Sook's poem to be exceedingly excellent with implied meaning reverberating in the final line. We must regard these two poems as top rate."

He continued, "At first glance, I could not judge which poem was best, but when I savored them again I can minutely judge their merits. Charan's poetic notion is so profound that one would extol [the poem] and dance [with delight] before even realizing it. The other poems are also all very clear and good, but only Unyŏng's displays a feel of vivid loneliness and yearning for a lover. I do not know who this person you think of is. Although

---

seventh lunar month.

[26] Musan (C. Wushan) is a well-known mountain in China that has often appeared in poetry and usually indicates a sexual relation between a man and woman. The mountain is said to be the abode of heavenly fairies, and the rain, clouds, and mountain itself are associated with the aforementioned legend of the pleasure of clouds and rain. The clouds in this line are a metaphor for Unyŏng's mind or desire.

[27] While the text refers to Changan (C. Changan), the long-time capital city of Chinese dynasties such as Han and Tang, in this instance it indicates the Chosŏn capital of Hanyang.

[28] The late Tang is the last of the aforementioned poetic periods of the Tang dynasty, extending from the time after the reign of Wenzong (827–840) until the fall of the dynasty some some eighty years later. Kŭnbo is the pen name of Sŏng Sammun mentioned above.

[29] The style of the poem by Pich'wi can be compared to a poem written and recited in a sonorous and elegant style (*soa*).

I must question about this, I will leave it for a while, for I cherish your talent."

At once, I went down to the garden, lay prostrate, and while crying answered, "It just came out by chance when I was writing the poem. How can there be another reason? Since now the Grand Prince doubts me, even if I died ten thousand times it would not be regrettable."

The Grand Prince ordered me to be seated and said, "As poems are what one has in one's mind, they are not something that can be covered or hidden. Do not say that again."

He then had ten bolts of silk brought out and divided among the ten of us. The Grand Prince had never set his mind on me, but all the palace people thought that he had.

The ten [of us] all retired to the rooms in the east. There a tall candle was lit, and on a cloisonné desk lay a volume of Tang rhymes. In the volume were the sorrowful poems of palace women, written long ago.[30] The palace women, except for me, debated the merits of these poems. Alone, I leaned against a folding screen, sitting dejectedly and not speaking, like a person made of mud. Sook turned and looked at me, saying, "Are you not speaking because you are worried after the Grand Prince doubted you for the poem you composed? Or rather is it because you are pleased with the joy of sharing love with the Grand Prince under the silken blanket [and do not want to speak of your good feelings]? There is no way I can know what you have in your mind."

I gathered my collar around my neck and answered, "You are not I. How can you know my mind? Just now, I thought of a poem and was about to write it, but I could not come up with a novel wording. That is the only reason I was quiet."

Ŭnsŏm then spoke. "Since your mind is not following your intent, you take the words of the person near you as the wind brushing by your ear. Seeing you as such, it is not difficult to figure out why you are so quiet. Let me demonstrate with a test."

Ŭnsŏm then demanded that I, using some grapes outside the window as my poetic theme, compose a poem. I responded directly with this poem:

The zigzagging vines are like a dragon moving about,
In the shadow of the verdurous leaves dwells a
sudden sentiment.

[30] These are the *kungwŏn si*, poems of bitterness and heartbreak written by palace women.

The harsh summer sunbeams illumine intensely,
The clear sky [juxtaposed] on the cold shadow is vainly bright.
Vines entangle the railing as if they have affection,
Ripened fruit, dangling like pearls, displays devotion.
Earnestly awaiting the day it will change of itself,
Riding on rain-laden clouds, it will rise to Samch'ŏng Palace.[31]

Sook read the poem, bowed, and said, "Truly you are an extraordinary talent. Similar to the ancient rhymes, the resonance of the poem is not high, but you composed the poem quickly, which is considered the most difficult thing for a poet to do. I am deeply pleased and willingly submit myself [to your talent] just like the seventy disciples submitted to Confucius."

Charan spoke. "Words should be restrained; why are you excessively praising the poem? It is only that some of her phrases are periphrastic and there is a soaring quality to the work."

The others heard this and responded, "That is a most proper comment."

Although my fellow palace women's doubts about me dissipated with this poem, it was not a case of all people thinking as such.

The following day I heard the clamorous noise of carts outside. The gatekeeper came in, informing us, "Many guests have arrived."

The Grand Prince had the East Pavilion cleaned and the guests ushered in; all were men of letters and talent. After all were shown to their seats, the Grand Prince showed them the poems we composed; all were greatly surprised, exclaiming, "It is as if we are unexpectedly seeing verses from the golden age of Tang again.[32] These are not something we can match. How did you come upon this most valuable treasure?"

Wearing a smile, the Grand Prince answered, "How can that be so? A boy servant picked those up on the street by chance. While I do not know who composed them, I think it must have come from the hand of a talented person of a commoner family."[33]

Several of the group could not dispel their doubts, and a bit later Sŏng Sammun said, "Talent is not something you can borrow

[31] Samch'ong or the Three Purities, are the three abodes of Daoist fairies, namely the palaces of Okch'ŏng, Sangch'ŏng, and T'aech'ŏng.

[32] This refers to the aforementioned Cheng-tang period of poetry in Tang China.

[33] The text reads *yŏyŏm*, referring to the areas where clusters of commoner houses would be.

from a different age. From the previous dynasty until now,[34] for over six hundred years the number of those in our country who distinguished their names through poetry is so enormous it cannot be surmised. However, some [poets] are turbid and thus not refined. Others are cheerful and are clear but wander; in general, the tones and rhymes are not in unison and the poetic nature lost. I do not desire to look upon such writing. Now, looking at these poems, [we can see that] the poetic nature is clear and sincere, and the thought and intent are outstanding. There is not even a small trace of the mundane world in the poems. These poems are inevitably of ones who live at the palace never in contact with the vulgar people outside [the palace], ones who read and recite the poetry of the ancients day and night, and have learned it by heart. If one is to savor the meaning of the poems intently, the phrase 'in the wind, alone, disillusioned and sad' holds the meaning of longing for one's lover, and the line 'a solitary bamboo stands, never losing its green hue' carries the meaning of maintaining one's fidelity. Also, the line 'my deepest thought is yearning for the lord of Zhou' shows sincerity for the king. As for the phrases 'becoming dewdrop beads, it remains on the lotus leaf' and 'to the western mountain peak and the brook at its front,' if these were not written by fairies from the heavens there is no means to describe them. Although there are both merits and demerits in the rhythm, a nature imbued with virtue and righteousness is largely the same [in each of the poems]. You have undoubtedly fostered ten heavenly fairies at this palace, lord; I entreat you to deceive me no longer."

The Grand Prince, while being moved with admiration in his heart, outwardly did not nod his head and replied, "Who said that Kŭnbo has the ability to appraise poems? How can there be such persons within this palace? Your suspicions are too extreme."

At that time, the ten of us were watching quietly through a crack in the window, and among us, there were none not impressed [at Sŏng's compliment].

That night Charan sincerely spoke to me wholeheartedly, asking, "As we were born women, our parents all wish for us to have families. Although I do not know what kind of person you have in mind as a lover, daily your countenance grows more haggard.

[34] The previous dynasty referred to here is that of Koryŏ, which held power over the Korean peninsula from 918 to 1392.

Now I worry about this and sincerely ask of you: please do not hide even a bit and tell me what troubles you."

I got up and thanked her, and began to tell her what had happened.

"There are many people about the palace, and I feared that someone would overhear me and gossip, so I dared not open my mouth. Yet, as you ask me with such friendship, how can I keep this hidden? At the time last fall when the chrysanthemums were in bloom and the foliage had begun to change colors, the Grand Prince sat alone in the *sŏdang*. He ordered a maidservant to grind down an ink-stick and unfurl a silk [scroll]. He then wrote ten verses on it. At that time, a boy servant came in and announced, 'There is a young scholar claiming to be Kim *chinsa*, and he would like an audience with you.'

"The Grand Prince greeted the scholar, who was dressed in hempen clothes and wearing a leather belt. He came up the stone steps briskly, appearing like a bird unfolding its wings. He came in, bowed, and sat down. His countenance was like that of a Daoist ascetic.[35] The Grand Prince looked at him once and was inclined toward him, quickly changing seats so as to face Kim. The *chinsa* rose from his seat and said in gratitude, 'Impertinently I have received much warm favor [from you] and yet shamefully have not accepted your invitation. I cannot put into words how overwhelmed I am to be here now and see you greet me with pleasure.'

"The Grand Prince consoled him [saying], 'For long I have heard of and respected your fame; now that I sit here and receive your greeting, felicity fills this house. This house becomes glorious as much as if I had gained a hundred friends.'

"When the *chinsa* had entered, he had already seen us. However, since he was a young scholar, the Grand Prince held him comfortably in his heart and thus did not order us to move out of the room. The Grand Prince looked at the *chinsa*, saying, 'The autumn scenery is very fine. I wish that you would write one new verse and so bathe this house in luster.'

"The *chinsa* moved from his seat, declining: 'My fame is but vanity and has no essence. How could I boldly know the rhythm of a poem?'

---

[35] The text reads *sinsŏn*, implying an otherworldly being.

"The Grand Prince had Kŭmnyŏn sing, Puyong play the *kŏmun'go*, Poryŏn play the *tanso*, Pigyŏng hold a drinking cup, and me hold the inkstone.[36] I was only a young woman at that time.[37] When I looked at the *chinsa* once, I felt dizzy and my heart thumped. While the *chinsa* looked at me, he smiled and often eyed me carefully.

"The Grand Prince looked at the *chinsa*, saying, 'I have truly received you with great hospitality. How can you impertinently begrudge one verse and bring shame to this house?'

"Thereupon, the *chinsa* grasped the writing brush and composed a verse:[38]

As the wild geese fly toward the south,
The autumn colors are deep in the palace.
As the water becomes colder, the lotus blossoms lose
  their beauty, and
Chrysanthemums heavy with frost droop in the golden light.
On the silk cushion is a rose-cheeked beauty,
From the lute rises the "Song of White Snow."[39]
With one measure of violet sky-colored liquor,[40]
First drunken, worries are washed from my mind.

"The Grand Prince recited this several times and said with surprise, 'Truly you have what is called extraordinary talent. Why have we met so late?'

"The ten of us at once looked at one another, and with surprise said in accord, 'This must be the heavenly sage Wang Zijin who came down from heaven![41] If not, how can such a person be explained?'

"The Grand Prince, while offering a cup of wine to the *chinsa* queried, 'Among the poets of old, who do you think is the master?'

---

36 The *kŏmun'gŏ* is a six-stringed zither and the *tanso* a small-notched flute.

37 The text reads *so yŏja*, indicating an age of sixteen to twenty. Other texts, particularly the copy used by Yi Sanggu (1999), states she was sixteen.

38 A pentasyllabic verse of eight lines.

39 "Paeksŏl-gok" (C. "Baixue-qu") is a famous song of the Chinese Chu kingdom (704–202 BCE).

40 *Yuha-chu*, the liquor taken by heavenly fairies.

41 Wang Zijin was the crown prince of King Ling of Zhou. For speaking frankly to the king, he was reduced in status to an illegitimate son (*soin*). A legend concerning him states that he was fond of wandering about and playing his flute, said to sound like the cry of a phoenix. One day while doing so he met a Daoist sage and became a heavenly being able to ride to the heavens on the back of a crane.

"The *chinsa* replied, 'In my opinion, Li Bo was a heaven-sent sage; he must have been long near the incense altar of the Jade Emperor and then come down to Mt. Kunlun for enjoyment.[42] There, he drank all the jade elixir[43] and unable to overcome his drunken exhilaration, he held a jewel-like flower and broke off a ten thousand year-old tree branch, rode on the wind, and fell to this human world. Lu Zhao-rin and Wang Bo were heavenly beings from above the seas, and their poetry was in harmony with the rise and fall of the sun and moon, the changing of the clouds, the roll of the blues waves, the spouting of whales, the boundless expanse of islands, luxuriant grasses and trees, lotus flowers and water chestnut leaves, songs of waterfowl, and the tears of serpents, all of which they embraced in their hearts. Meng Hao-ran, who learned tones and rhymes from Master Kuang, had the most elegant tones. Li Yi-shan learned the magic arts of the sages from early on and conjured forth a wondrous poetic creative power. His life's writings are no more than the words of a ghost [i.e., of a person from another world]. All of the other poets have their own special characteristics. How can I speak of them all?'[44]

"The Grand Prince responded, 'Every day when the literary men and I debate poetry, Du Fu is most commonly named as the best poet. Why do you state [differently]?'

---

42 Mt. Kunlun (K. Kollyun-san) is a mountain in China where heavenly fairies are said to dwell.

43 Jade elixir (K. *ogaek*) refers to the juice that comes from jade. Drinking this enables long life, and thus it is claimed to be a magical elixir.

44 Lao Zhao-rin (637–689?) was a renowned literary man of the early Tang dynasty, and along with Wang Bo (650–676), Yang Jiong (650–700?), and Luo Binwang (650–684) is acclaimed as one of the four great literary talents of the period. He suffered from epilepsy for a long period and eventually took his own life by jumping into a river because of his depression.

Wang Bo is acclaimed as a great poet of the early Tang dynasty. He died early while crossing the sea.

Meng Hao-ran (689–740) was a poet of Tang China and is acclaimed particularly as a master of the *oŏn-si* (pentasyllabic poems).

Master Kuang was a musician in the Jin kingdom during the Warring States period (475–221 BCE). He is said to have been able to discriminate delicate tones and even able to predict good or bad fortune by listening to sounds.

Li Yi-shan is the courtesy name of the Tang poet Li Shang-yin (813–858). He was driven to write poetry by a poetry ghost (*sima*). We find a similar sentiment described by other poets, especially Yi Kyubo (1168–1241), who wrote a prose piece titled "Ku sima-mun" [Writing to drive away a poetry ghost] that is recorded in his literary collection *Tongguk Yisangguk chip* [Collected works of Minister Yi of the Eastern Country].

"The *chinsa* answered, 'If we only talk about what the ordinary Confucians venerate, that is same as saying raw meat and roasted meat are pleasing to the people's mouths. Zimei's poems are deliberately raw meat and roasted meat.'[45]

"The Grand Prince rebutted, 'He mastered all literary styles and was especially exquisite at poetic skills such as metaphor and allusion.[46] Why do you hold Du Fu so insignificant?'

"The *chinsa* apologized and said, 'How could I dare regard him lightly? Regarding his major qualities, these can be likened to Emperor Wu going to Weiyang Palace and becoming enraged at all the barbarians invading the four quarters, and thus ordering his generals to strike the enemy;[47] his merits are the same as a million troops with the strength of a bear extending out over a thousand leagues.[48] Regarding the minor aspects, it is like having Sima Xiangru compose "Changmen fu" or having Sima Qian compose "Fengshan-wen." Seeking a heavenly being, it is like Dongfang Shuo serving [Emperor Wu] while Xiwang-mu offers [the emperor] a heavenly peach.[49] Thus, the writings of Du Fu can be

---

[45] Zimei is the courtesy name of Du Fu.

[46] The preface to the *Sijing* [Book of songs] explains, "There are six classes: first, the Fung (*p'ung*); second, descriptive pieces (*pu*); third, metaphorical pieces (*pi*); fourth, allusive pieces (*hŭng*), fifth, the Ya (*a*); and sixth the Sung (*song*)." See James Legge, *The Chinese Classics*, vol. 4, *The She King*, 34–35. Of the six, *pu*, *pi*, and *hŭng* seem to be styles or modes of writing as indicated by the English glosses. The other three classes are explained by Legge as types of writing. In this case, the text, in the voice of the Grand Prince, informs us that Du Fu was a master of *pi* and *hŭng*, or metaphor and allusion.

[47] Emperor Wu reigned from 141 to 87 BCE in the Former Han dynasty (202–9 CE). Weiyang Palace, located in the western area of Changan, is a famous palace of the Han dynasty.

[48] I use the rather ambiguous Western measure of distance "league" for the equally indeterminate *li* used in the text.

[49] Sima Xiangru (179–117 BCE) was a literary man of the Former Han dynasty who gained fame during the rule of the aforementioned Emperor Wu for his diplomacy with the barbarians in the south and for his literary skills.

The prose-poem "Changmen fu" [Prose-poem of Changmen] (the text reads "Fu Changyang") was written by Sima Xiangru on behalf of Empress Chen. The empress was initially favored by Emperor Wu but fell out of favor and was exiled to Changmen Palace. She contracted Sima to write "Changmen fu" on her behalf, and when the emperor read this work, he realized his error and again brought the empress back to his side.

Sima Qian (?-86? BCE) is a historian of the Former Han dynasty and was best known for compiling *Siji* [Records of the historian].

"Fengshan-wen" [Writing of the earthen altar] is one of the eight *sŏ* (writings) included in the *Siji*. "Fengshan" refers to the ceremony offered to the heavens and earth by the Chinese emperor and is a record concerning the spirits of the royal ancestral shrine (Chongmyo).

said to fulfill all sort of literary styles. However, if compared with Li Bo, it is the same as the heavens and earth not being comparable and a river and the sea not being the same. If Du Fu drives his cart from the front, Wang Wei[50] and Meng Hao-ran compete on the road while brandishing the whip [and driving the horses] from behind.'

"The Grand Prince replied, 'Hearing your words, I feel my bosom is opened in a brief instant, and I am enraptured as if I were riding a long breeze up to T'aech'ong Palace.[51] Although Du Fu's poetry is imbued with heaven's grandness, it is deficient for expressing passions and customs.[52] How can it thus be compared with that of Wang Wei and Meng Hao-ran? Beyond this debate, however, I now ask you to compose a poem once more to fill this house with even more luminosity.' The *chinsa* directly wrote a poem-song, on peach-blossom paper:

On the golden pond smoke scatters and the touch of dew
  is crisp,
The azure sky is clear as water, why is the night so long?
The gentle breeze blows aside the beaded blind with purpose,
The bright moon with its deep affection enters the small room.
When the shade at the edge of the garden is opened,
  a pine regains its shadow,
The wine in the cup undulates and holds the fragrance
  of chrysanthemums.
Although Duke Yuan[53] is young, he drinks exceedingly well,

Dongfang Shuo lived during the time of Emperor Wu of the Former Han dynasty. He served in the Han government and was renowned for his humor and eloquence in speech. Legend tells that he stole and ate the heavenly peach of Xiwang-mu and thus was able to achieve immortality.

Xiwang-mu (Queen Mother of the West) is a heavenly fairy that assisted the rulers of ancient China. Her surname was Yang and given name Hui. When King Mu of the Zhou kingdom (1027–771 BCE) was hunting on the western slopes of Mt. Kunlun he met Xiwang-mu, and they enjoyed each other's company so much that they forgot to return. Also, and perhaps more germane to Dongfang Shuo, when Emperor Wu of the Former Han dynasty wished for longevity, she held him to be commendable and came down from the heavens with seven heavenly peaches (*sŏndo*) and gave them to him.

50 Wang Wei (699–759) was a poet, a skilled musician, and a landscape painter of the Tang period.

51 T'aech'ŏng Palace is one of the aforementioned Samch'ŏng (i.e., the three abodes of Daoist fairies) where the heavenly fairies reside.

52 The text reads that the work is not sufficient for *akpu,* that is, poetry for expressing human passions and customs.

53 Yuan Ji (210–263 CE) of the Wei kingdom (220–265 CE). Accounts tell that Yuan was very fond of drink and also played the six-stringed zither well.

Do not think it odd, being drunk between jugs of liquor
and then mad.

"The Grand Prince thought this all the more extraordinary and while sitting closer [to the *chinsa*] he grasped his hand, saying, '*Chinsa,* you are not a talent of this world, and thus, I cannot appraise the quality [of your poems]. It is not only your ability in prose and brushwork, but also the innate wonderfulness. It was not by chance that heaven sent you to be born in the Eastern Quarter [i.e., Chosŏn].'

"The Grand Prince again had the *chinsa* brush his calligraphy. While the writing brush was fluttering in the hand of the *chinsa,* a drop of ink splattered on my finger. I thought this honorable and did not wash it away. The palace attendants of the left and right gazed upon this, smiling broadly and likening it to a gateway for success.[54] Shortly it grew late, and the water clock[55] announced the lateness. The Grand Prince, while sleepily stretching, said, 'I am drunk. Let us retire and rest, but do not forget: When the morning is bright, if you have an inkling, bring a *kŏmun'go* and come again.'

"The next day the Grand Prince again read the two poems and said admiringly, 'Surely he can contend for supremacy with Kunbo, but in his refined deportment, he surpasses him.'

"From that time on, although I lay down I could not sleep, my heart was so tormented that I could not eat any meals, and I did not know even if my clothes kept me warm. Do you not remember?"

Charan replied, "I guess I had forgotten about that. Now that I hear you speak, it as if I have sobered up after drinking, and a hazy memory has returned."

After that, the Grand Prince frequently met the *chinsa,* but we were not able to see each other. Thus, I would always spy through a chink in the door. One day, on fine, snow-white writing paper, I wrote a verse:

---

54 The text reads *tŭng yong mun* "climbing to Yongmun." Yongmun (C. Longmen) is a mountain upstream of the Huanghe River. Legend states that if a carp swims upstream to this place it will transform into a dragon. Thus this phrase was used as a metaphor for achieving success or good fortune.

55 The *kyŏngnu* (clepsydra) used dripping water to mark the passage of time during the night. Because of the massive size and expense of these devices, it seems that the water clock mentioned in the text was located at the main palace.

The scholar dressed in hempen clothes and girded
with a leather belt,
His jade-like countenance seems as a heavenly sage.
Even if always through the bead blinds, I see him,
Why is there no destiny [for us] beneath the moon?[56]
Washing my face, my tears become water,
Plucking the *kŏmun'go,* my deep sorrow cries from the strings.
Holding my boundless sorrow within my breast,
Alone, I raise my head, appealing to the heavens.

I wrapped the poem in many folds along with a golden hairpin and sealed it, intending to give it to the *chinsa,* but there was no means to do so. That evening the Grand Prince prepared a drinking party to display the talent of the *chinsa* to his guests. The Grand Prince showed the two poems of the *chinsa,* which were read in turn with nonstop praise, and all wished to meet him. The Grand Prince at once sent a servant and a horse for the *chinsa.* Shortly thereafter, the *chinsa* arrived and was seated. However, his face was gaunt, and his vigor seemed to have vanished altogether; his appearance was very different.

The Grand Prince comforted him, "*Chinsa,* you do not yet have the worries of the Chu kingdom;[57] did you become so emancipated walking around a pond beforehand?"

All the guests laughed loudly at this. The *chinsa* rose and bowed, saying, "I, a humble scholar, impertinently have received the favor of the Grand Prince. Perhaps because of the passing of good fortune and the onset of calamity, illness has bound my body, and I am unable to eat or drink. I even had to rely upon another for moving about. Today, as I have received your generous summons, I have come to pay my respects while being supported by another."

Thereupon, all the seated guests shifted their knees and paid him deep respect. As he was the youngest [among the gathered

---

[56] This line reads *ha mu wŏl ha yŏn,* referring to the destiny of love between men and women controlled by the Old Man Beneath the Moon (Wŏlha noin). The usage here indicates the desire of Unyŏng for Kim *chinsa.*

[57] The text reads *u ch'o chi sim* [a heart/mind with the worries of the Chu kingdom]). The story behind this phrase concerns Qu Yuan (343?–277?), a minister of the Chu kingdom. Qu was exiled by the king and went to the Miluoshui River, where he worried greatly about the country and eventually killed himself in the river in his agitated state. The Grand Prince uses this analogy for the *chinsa* since he has not entered Chosŏn officialdom and thus does not have to worry about the well-being of the country or the king.

scholars], the *chinsa* took the seat farthest away [from the center]; there was only a single wall separating us from the inner room where I stayed. It was soon deep into the night, and all the guests were quite drunk. When I made a hole in the wall and peeped inside, the *chinsa* knew the meaning of this and sat facing the corner. I cast the sealed letter through the hole, and the *chinsa* grasped it and returned to his house. When he opened and read it, he could not endure the sorrow in his heart, and, for all the world, could not let go of the letter in his hand. It seemed that the longing and yearning in his heart toward me was even greater than ever, and it became difficult to simply survive. Although he directly wrote a reply to send to me, there was no messenger to entrust the letter with, and he was alone in worry and lamentation.

One day he heard rumor of a shaman who lived outside the East Gate and had gained fame through her supernatural ability. She also visited Susŏng Palace, where she was trusted and held in favor. Thus, the *chinsa* went to her house to meet her. She was not yet thirty and quite beautiful. She had become a widow at an early age and of her own accord behaved as a lewd woman.[58] Seeing the *chinsa* coming to her place, she treated him to a grand table of liquor and food. He took hold of a cup and without drinking said, "Today I have an urgent task, but I will return tomorrow."

The next day he also went and she again cordially treated him. Yet he could not boldly ask favor and said again, "I will come again tomorrow."

The shaman, seeing the unworldliness of the *chinsa*'s face, was pleased in her mind. However, as the *chinsa* had visited her day after day but did not speak a word, she thought it was probably because he was a young man too shy to speak coarsely [of his desire] to her. She decided that she would first entice him and then hold him until nightfall, whereupon she would demand that he sleep with her.

The next day after bathing, the shaman put on thick makeup and beautifully adorned herself with various ornaments. She prepared the bed with blankets perfumed with flowers and put

---

[58] *Mudang* (*munyŏ*) were considered by official society to be lewd women (*ŭmnyŏ*) by virtue of their trade, their mingling with men, and their lifestyle. Based on the behavior of this particular shaman later in the narrative, it seems the label "lewd" is applied because of her unchaste lifestyle.

out a jeweled floor cushion. She then sent a young maid outside the gate to wait for him. The *chinsa* again came and, looking at her face, magnificent clothes, and the beautiful trappings set out, thought it quite strange.

The shaman spoke enticingly, "What kind of evening is it to see such an excellent person as you tonight?"

Since the *chinsa* had no intentions toward the shaman, he did not answer and instead stood with a troubled countenance. Angered, she asked, "Why is a young man like you not reluctant to frequently visit a widow's house?"

He responded, "If you have supernatural ability, how come you haven't figured out why I am here?"

The shaman at once went to her altar room[59] and bowed to the spirits. She shook her bell-rattle and invoked the gods; her body then quivered, and the spirits made a series of mysterious sounds [through her]. After some while she turned around and said, "Ah, you are truly pitiful! As you are not only trying to accomplish a difficult scheme to achieve your desire, but doing so in an unsuitable manner, you will certainly fail and within three years become one of the next world."

The *chinsa,* with tears flowing, expressed his gratitude: "Even if you said nothing, I already knew everything. However, the sorrow pent up in my heart cannot be resolved even with medicine of every kind. If through you I could only convey this letter to her, even death would be glorious."

The shaman replied, "With this lowborn body, although I sometimes visit the palace to perform rites,[60] I dare not go unless I am summoned. However, I will try for you."

He took an envelope from under his shirt and gave it to the shaman, saying, "I beg you to be careful. If this is given to the wrong person a calamity will rise like no other."

The shaman took the letter and entered the palace gate. The people in the palace all thought her coming to the palace strange, but the shaman explained herself resolutely. Stealing a chance, she took me to a place where none were around and gave me the letter. I returned to my room, tore open the letter; the contents read,

---

[59] The *yŏngjwa* is the room for the altar and paintings of the deities where the shaman would conduct most of her rituals.

[60] *Sinsa* are rites conducted to various deities for the benefit of humans. Generally, this term indicates rites conducted by shamans.

> From the time we bound our destiny with one look, my heart has grown restless, my spirit has gone out, and my mind cannot be easily pacified. Every time I look west of the palace,[61] it seems as if my bowels have been severed. With the letter that you passed me the other day through the wall, I humbly received your beautiful and unforgettable writing. Before I could unfold the whole letter, my breath was taken away, and before I finished half the letter, my tears had drenched the writing. From that time, I could not sleep although I lay down and I could not swallow any food although I tried to eat. Illness has touched the deepest part of my chest, and no sort of medicine will revive me. May heaven consider me pitiful and may ghosts help me silently. If ever, once in my life, my sorrow is relieved, I will purposely grind my body and make powder of my bones, and present rites to the myriad spirits in this world under heaven. While writing this letter, a lump binds my throat; what else can I say further?

At the end of the letter was the following poem:

> The gate to the deep and vast pavilion is closed for the day,
> The shadows of the trees and clouds are dim and vague.
> The flowers fallen on the flowing water drift away on a streamlet,
> A young swallow carrying mud returns to the edge of the eves.
> Leaning on my pillow, I cannot even dream of the butterfly,[62]
> In my lonely room, alone with deep sorrow, even an osprey would be rare.
> Your jade-like face is right before my eyes, but why are you not saying anything?
> At even the cry of orioles in the green forest, I soak my collar with tears.

After I had read the entire poem, my voice was dead and my heart lost. When my tears were exhausted, my blood became tears [and continued to flow]. Afraid someone might notice me, I hid myself behind a folding screen. From that time on I thought about him ever more, and I seemed like a stupid or mad person. As I could not hide myself through my words and appearance, it was not unreasonable for the Grand Prince to doubt me. Charan, likewise a woman with pent-up rancor and heartbreak, heard this

---

[61] That is, the location of Susŏng Palace.

[62] The dream of the butterfly (*hojŏp-mong*) refers to the dream that Zhuangzi (365–290 BCE) is said to have had. In his dream he became a butterfly and was thus able to fly about seeking pleasure.

tale and sobbed, saying, "As poems come from the sincere nature of one's heart, they cannot be used for deceit."

One day the Grand Prince summoned Pich'wi [and said], "There are ten of you in one place and thus you cannot study unhindered. Five of you should move to the Western Palace."

The same day, Charan, Ŭnsŏm, Pich'wi, Onggyŏ, and I moved to the Western Palace. After we arrived, Onggyŏ said, "Secluded flowers, fine grasses, flowing water, a lovely forest, and a fragrant grove—it is just like a mountain cottage or a farmer's hut in a field. This will truly be an excellent study place."

I replied, "We are neither scholars nor nuns who cultivate the Way, but nonetheless are still confined in this secluded palace. This place truly deserves to be called Changsin Palace."[63]

Hearing my words, all of our attendants sighed and were depressed. After this, I wrote a letter conveying my heart to the *chinsa* and waited to entrust it to the shaman. However, in the end, she did not come [to the palace] until the last moment, probably because she was upset to know that the *chinsa*'s heart was not for her.

One night, Charan secretly said to me, "Every year in the eighth lunar month the palace attendants all go to the brook beneath T'angch'un Terrace to do laundry and then afterward hold a feast.[64] It would be a good idea this year for us to try to hold this event in the Sogyŏksŏ district and seek out the shaman in the process of going to or returning from the event."[65]

---

[63] Changsin Palace (C. Changxin) was a royal palace of the Han dynasty and located deep within Changle Palace.

[64] *Chungch'u* falls in mid-autumn by the lunar calendar.

T'angch'un-dae is an elevated ground in Sŏdaemun-gu, Seoul City. It became infamous when Yŏnsan-gun (r. 1495–1596), the tenth king of Chosŏn, erected a pavilion on this spot and summoned numerous young women for merrymaking. It was renamed Yŏnyung-dae in 1754 by royal order; see *Yŏngjo sillok* [Veritable records of King Yŏngjo], 82:16b (1754-09-02).

Wansa is the task of laundering silk and other items of the palace women.

[65] Sogyŏksŏ-dong is the present-day Samch'ŏng-dong, of Chongno-gu, Seoul City. In the Chosŏn period there was an office there with the same name that was charged with performing rites to the sun, moon, and stars. Here Daoist rites were also given to the deities of the Samch'ŏng (the Three Purities), the three heavenly abodes of Daoist fairies. The office was present from the early days of Chosŏn and renamed Sogyŏksŏ in 1466 but was abolished in 1518; subsequently it was reestablished in 1525, but abolished for good after the Hideyoshi invasions of 1592–1598. See *Han'guk minsok taesajŏn*, 2:859.

I thought that a good idea and impatiently waited for the eighth month. Each day seemed like three years. Pich'wi had secretly eavesdropped on our conversation, and while deliberately pretending not to know, asked me, "When you first came [to the palace], your face shone like a plum blossom, and even without makeup you had a naturally beautiful appearance; for that reason the palace attendants called you 'Lady Kwikkuk.'[66] Recently, your countenance does not shine as in the past and gradually your beauty has declined. What is the reason for this?"

I replied, "My disposition has always been weak. Every steamy and hot season I am always lethargic and become gaunt. When the paulownia leaves begin to fall and cool temperatures come in through the curtains, I will be better."

Pich'wi then wrote and gave me a single verse of a playful poem. Although it was intended to make fun of me, its poetic sentiment was exquisite. While I held her talent in esteem, I was embarrassed with her jesting.

Somehow or other, some months passed, and autumn began to approach. In the evenings a cool breeze arose, chrysanthemums emitted a golden-yellow hue, the sound of hundreds of insects echoed, and from the white moon flowed bright light. Inside, I was delighted that it was finally autumn, but did not express this elation in words.

Ŭnsŏm said to me, "A good season for delivering a letter is not far off. The joy of the human world—how can it be different from that of the heavens?"

Hearing this, I knew that I could no longer deceive those of the Western Palace and straightforwardly said, "I pray that you do not let those of the Southern Palace know of this."

Since geese were heading south and round, jewel-like drops of dew were forming, it was the very season to do laundry in the clear water. With many other palace women, we tried to set a date for going to the stream but could not reach an accord on where to go. Those from the Southern Palace insisted, "There is no better place than below T'anch'un Terrace, which has clear water and white rocks."

However, those of the Western Palace insisted, "The scenery of

---

66 Lady Kwikkuk (C. Lady Guoguo) was the older sister of Queen Yanggue (719–756) and became the favorite queen of Emperor Xuanzong (r. 712–756).

Sogyŏksŏ district is not inferior to that of T'anch'un Terrace. Why do you abandon the closer place and seek a further spot?

Still, those of the Southern Palace stubbornly held their position and would not concur with us. As an agreement was not reached by nightfall we all dispersed. That night, Charan spoke to me, saying, "Among the five at the Southern Palace, Sook has the most influential opinion, and among us five here at the Western Palace, I carry the most weight. Let me try to change her mind with a scheme."

She summoned a young maidservant, and with a jade lantern lighting the road she alone went to the Southern Palace. Kŭmnyŏn happily greeted her, "Once we were separated into the Southern and Western palaces, we became estranged like the Qin and Chu kingdoms.[67] As you have unexpectedly honored us with your presence here tonight, I am very thankful."

Then Sook said, "What are you thankful for? She is no more than a guest who has come to change our minds."

Charan straightened her collar, and with a serious look said, "Oh, so you can read what another has in her mind? Then speak of it [my intent]!"

Sook responded, "While those of the Western Palace want to go to Sogyŏksŏ, I alone am unbendingly set against that. For that reason you visit us in the middle of night. Isn't it correct that you came here to change our minds?"

Charan replied, "Out of the five of us at the Western Palace, I alone intend to go inside the city gates [to Sogyŏksŏ]."

Sook asked, "For what reason are you alone considering going inside the city gates [to Sogyŏksŏ]?"

Charan answered, "Listen to me. I've heard that Sogyŏksŏ was the place where rites were offered to the heavenly emperor and was thus called the Samch'ŏng District. Surely, we were all fairies of Samch'ŏng Palace, but exiled to the human world for misreading the *Hwangjŏng sutra*.[68] Since we are already in the mundane world, any place I live—a mountain cottage, village, farm, or fishing hamlet—does not matter to me. However, while being confined resolutely in the deep palace like a bird in a bamboo cage, I lament at the sound of a golden oriole's song and even sob

[67] Qin and Chu were two strong kingdoms of the Chinese Warring States period (475–221 BCE) and became estranged through poor relations, with Qin eventually destroying Chu in 223 BCE.

[68] The *Hwangjŏng sutra* [Sutra of the Yellow Court; C. *Huangting jing*] is one of the main sutras of Daoism. The author is not known.

at the [sight of a] green willow. Even worse, I feel so lonely to see swallows flying in pairs or dozing birds roosting face to face. Among the grasses, there are those that intertwine, and among trees, there are those that join roots.[69] Even ignorant grasses and trees and lowly birds have the joy of innate yin and yang. What sin have the ten of us alone committed that we must be fettered to this isolated and lonely palace, while the spring flowers and autumn moon pass? Always oppressed by false rules—why are we destined to such a cruel fate? As once a person is old he or she can never again be young, think again, how can I not be sad! At Sogyŏksŏ, I will cleanse my body in a clear brook, and then go to T'aeŭl Shrine,[70] where I will make one hundred bows so deep my head touches the ground and pray to Buddha with my hands clasped. I am only trying to save my next life from such hardship. What other intention could I have? We palace women had a bond like siblings. Because of this one thing, why should we wrongfully become suspicious of each other? It is because of my rudeness that I have not gained your confidence."

Sook rose and apologized. "Compared with you, I am not enlightened to good reason. I did not at first agree with going inside the city gates [to Sogyŏksŏ] for our gathering because there are crowds of scoundrels and adventurers about, and I feared that there could be an unexpected disgrace. As such, I doubted your [suggestion]. Now, hearing your words, I see good reason. How could one understanding such reasoning not go to the village [i.e., Sogyŏksŏ]? From now on, even if you say you will rise to the heavens in the daylight or you will cross the sea without a boat, I will follow you. For what we call humans and realizing their affairs successfully, there is no other way."

Then Puyong spoke. "In general, there ought to be consensus in matters; however, the last time when we talked about this we could not reach an agreement. As our master [i.e., the Grand Prince] does not know of all the matters of the house and we secretly deliberate among ourselves, this is nothing more than being disloyal. If we change our minds before the night is even half over about a matter that caused a quarrel in the day, this is

---

[69] This joining of the roots by two trees (*yŏlli*) is a symbol of deep love between husband and wife.

[70] T'aeŭl-sa is the shrine where rites to the deity T'aeŭl were offered. In Daoist beliefs, this deity is thought to have created all matter and mostly commonly resides in the North Star (i.e., Polaris). T'aeŭl is believed to govern calamity, life, and death.

the same as losing one's truthfulness. There is not a streamlet that is not jade-clear on an autumn day. It is not right that you insist upon going to only the place within the city walls [Sogyŏksŏ]. As the spot below T'angch'un Terrace has clear water and white rocks, it is where we do laundry every year. Now you wish to abruptly change to another spot, which is not right either. [To follow you] I will lose four things for one, and for that reason, I will not go with you all."

Next, Poryŏn spoke. "Speech is like an instrument to add luster to the body. Fortune and misfortune result from how one uses it in either a prudent or reckless manner. Cognizant of this, a person of virtue is careful with his words and keeps his mouth closed as a cork closes a bottle. In the Han dynasty, Bing Ji would not speak all day and still could accomplish any matter. Conversely, Se Fu was a skillful orator but still Zhang Shi-zhi exposed his fault to the monarch. [Considering this,] in Charan's words there is something she is hiding and did not reveal, Sook's speech is a case of being compelled to follow another, and Puyong's words are only efforts at embellishment. None of these are my intent, and accordingly I will not go on this outing."[71]

Then Kŭmnyŏn added, "Tonight's discussion will not see agreement; let me humbly offer a divination."

She opened the *Book of Changes*[72] and after the divination she began to explain the signs: "Tomorrow, without fail, Unyŏng will meet a man. As Unyŏng's face and carriage are not those of a person of this world, for a long time the Grand Prince's heart has been inclined toward her. Yet she will disobey him at the cost of her life for no other reason than she cannot shun the kindness of his wife. Even if the Grand Prince's order is strict, for fear she might be injured, he did not dare be close to her. Now, as she lives in this lonesome place and intends to go to such a lively

[71] Bing Ji was the prime minister during the reign of Emperor Xuan (74–49 BCE) of the Former Han dynasty. Se Fu was a local official of the Jin kingdom charged with legal matters and taxation. He was eventually forced out of office. Zhang Shi-zhi bought a position and served Emperor Wen (r. 180–157 BCE) of the Former Han dynasty. The contention between Zhang and Se Fu was about an appointment that Se was given as a result of his flattering words to Emperor Wen. Zhang objected, stating that if those who gave flattering words were the only ones rewarded, there would be no truthful speech. The emperor saw his error and did not give Se the position.

[72] The text states that she used the *Hŭigyŏng* [C. *Xijing*], which is another name for the *Yŏkkyŏng* [C. *Yijing*, The Book of Changes], one of the Five Confucian Classics. This work was used as a divination manual by Confucians.

place, if a young man with a heart for pleasure sees her beauty, he will inevitably lose his mind and go mad. Even if they do not come near each other, pointing at one another with their fingers and looking at each other are also disgraceful. The other day the Grand Prince commanded that if any one of us goes out of the palace gates or any outsider even knows our name, for these crimes, the punishment would be death. Thus, I will not take part in this event either."

Charan knew that she could not accomplish her task. Disappointed, she was cheerlessly on the verge of saying good night and returning [to the Western Palace]. However, while crying, Pigyŏng grasped her silk belt, forcibly held her back, and offered milk-cloud wine.[73] After the palace women in the room all drank it, Kŭmnyŏn spoke: "Tonight's gathering should have ended in a subdued mood, but the reason for Pigyŏng's tears is truly beyond me."

Pigyŏng replied, "When Unyŏng first came to the Southern Palace, we became very close and pledged [to remain so] in life or death, glory or honor. Now even though we live in different places, how can I forget that? The other day when I saw Unyŏng paying her respects to the Grand Prince, her slender waist had become even leaner, her face haggard, and her voice thread-thin as if nothing at all was coming out of her mouth. When she was rising to bow, in an instant, her strength vanished and she fell to the ground. As I helped her up and said something nice to solace her, she replied, 'Unfortunately I have become ill and will die shortly. There is nothing regrettable for the loss of a humble life as mine. However, the nine of you grow daily in literary skill and talent, and on a later day, your beautiful poems and fine works will impress and change the world. Since I will not be able to see this with my own eyes, I am deeply saddened.' Upon hearing her sad words, I wept. Now I think about this and realize that her illness is because of longing for her love. Oh woe! Charan is Unyŏng's true friend, and she is trying to put a person about to die on the altar before heaven. If the plan of today cannot be realized, it will cause her [i.e., Unyŏng] to go to the next world after death without being able to close her eyes.[74] This bitterness and

---

[73] *Unyu-ju*, a type of cloudy white liquor.

[74] Unyŏng would become a wandering spirit, one unable to fully pass to the next world because of lingering bitterness for the unfinished life in this world. In the shamanic worldview, a person dying with such a grudge would cause hardships and misfortune for those in this world.

sorrow would then certainly come to the Southern Palace, would it not? It is said, 'If one does one good thing, heaven will send down one hundred types of auspiciousness; if one does one bad thing, heaven will send down one hundred types of calamity.' Is today's discussion a good thing or a bad thing?"

Sook spoke again: "I have already consented and three others have followed my intent. Why would I change my mind in the midst [of the discussion]? Even if this matter is revealed, it is only Unyŏng that will suffer the penalty. What could possibly happen to the others? I will not speak two words and suffer death for the sake of Unyŏng."

Charan, who had been about to leave, remained to see how things worked out. Some, in particular Poryŏn, Kŭmnyŏn, and Puyong desired to go with the group, but were embarrassed to go back on the words they had spoken. Charan spoke again: "For the matters of the world there is a correct path and an expedient path; if the expedient path is right, that way is also correct. How can you not use the more flexible expedient way and simply cling to the words you first spoke?"

The three, at once, followed her.

Next, Pigyŏng spoke: "Long ago, Su Jin[75] took the six countries and combined them into one; now Charan has easily brought five people into submission—she is an eloquent speaker indeed."

Charan replied, "The leaders of the six countries gave the state seal to Su Jin; what will the five of you give to me?"

Kŭmnyŏn answered, "That is because the combining of the six countries was beneficial to them; but with our submission what benefit did you bring to us five?"

The others looked at each another and laughed loudly. Charan replied, "I am not such as eloquent speaker, but I have caused you all to discuss loyalty. There was no other way [to help Unyŏng]. Those of the Southern Palace are all virtuous and will allow Unyŏng to continue her life. How can I not be thankful?"

Then she rose and bowed before them twice. Sook also rose and bowed twice. Charan spoke, "In this matter of today, the five of you concur. As heaven is above and the earth below, and as a ghost watches [us] and the lamp brightly illuminates, how can there be a different intent tomorrow?"

---

[75] Su Jin (?–317 BCE) was a strategist of the Warring States period and responsible for negotiating the alliance between the six countries of this period that was realized in 333 BCE. He then served as prime minister for the allied states.

She then rose again and bowed before going out. The five all went out beyond the gate to see her off.

When she returned to tell me of this, I rose with the support of the wall near me and bowed twice to her to show my sincere gratitude, saying, "My mother and father gave me life, but you are the one who is saving my life. Before my body is buried in the ground, I swear that I will repay this favor."

We sat and waited for morning. After offering our greetings [to the wife of the Grand Prince] in the inner room, we withdrew to the central room where everyone gathered. Sook spoke to me, saying, "The heavens are bright and the water clear: it is precisely the correct time to do the laundry. Today it would be good to go to Sogyŏksŏ and put up a tent, wouldn't it?"

None of the other eight had anything else to say. I withdrew from the others and went into the Western Palace. There I took a white silk jacket and wrote of all the sorrows and heartbreaks stored in my whole being on it; then I folded the jacket and put it next to my breast. Deliberately I lagged behind with Charan and told the boy groom, "The shaman outside of the East Gate is the greatest miracle worker; I'll go to that place and ask what ails me."

The boy servant set off [for the shaman's house] as I had said. By using a whip constantly and finding the road, he brought me to the house of the shaman, where I politely implored, "I came here today only with the hope of meeting Kim *chinsa* once. If you could possibly tell him that I am here, I will repay this debt with all of my being."

The shaman sent a person as I asked, and the *chinsa* hurriedly came in. The two of us looked at each other, but could not speak even a word—only tears flowed down our faces. I gave him the letter saying, "In the evening I will surely return; please, my dearest, wait here for me."

Then I quickly mounted the horse and rode off. The *chinsa* opened my letter, which read,

> The letter recently given me by the fairy of Mt. Wushan[76] was filled with sonorous jade-like notes. Holding the letter with both hands, as I read and re-read it three times, I was filled with both sorrow and happiness. I hoped to directly send my response and

[76] While the text refers to the legend of the fairy on Mt. Wushan mentioned in an earlier note, in this instance it seems a metaphor for the shaman who delivered the letter to Unyŏng from Kim *chinsa*.

my embrace of love, but there was no one I could trust to convey this [to you]. Also, as I feared that this secret might be revealed, all I could do was crane my neck and look to a far-off place. Although I wanted to fly to you, as I do not have wings to do so, I felt as if my bowels had been pierced and my very spirit lost. I now only wait for death; before I die, into this letter I put all the sorrows my life has embraced, and I pray that my dearest will keep this in your mind. My home is in Honam.[77] My parents favored me most among my siblings so that I was trusted and on my own even when playing outside. Thus, every day I frolicked in the woods and on stream banks, and in the shade of bamboo stands and apricot, mandarin orange, and citron trees. The children fishing on the moss-covered rocks and those playing flutes after having tended the cows were before my eyes morning and evening. Not only that, but the scenery of the mountains and fields, the bustle of the farming villages, and such sights were as many as the hairs on my head, so that I cannot describe them all. When I was thirteen, the Grand Prince summoned me and separated me from my parents and siblings; I entered the palace, leaving my family a thousand leagues behind. At first, I could not suppress my heart and wished to return home. I went about with disheveled hair and filth stuck to my face so that those who saw me thought I was dirty. Yet the Grand Prince's wife loved me ever more, and the Grand Prince adored me as well. This humble body was favored most among all the palace women. Since I have known about moral righteousness and rapidly learned tones and rhymes after I devoted myself to study, the Grand Prince praised me for that as well. After moving to the Western Palace, I concentrated on only the *kŏmun'go* and letters,[78] and my knowledge became even deeper. There was not a single poem written by those noble guests [at the palace] that caught my eyes. Not being born a man, I could not rise in the world and gain fame, and as an unfortunate rose-cheeked woman, I was secluded in this deep palace for the ages. Because of this, bitterness has bound my mind, and [my] deep resentment could fill the ocean. This past autumn night when I saw your face, I felt in my heart that you were a heavenly being who had descended to this world. I am not any less pretty than the other nine [palace women]; from what destiny of a previous life would the single drop from your writing brush cause the onset of this bitterness and sorrow in my heart? Looking at you through the beaded blinds, I imagined my fate as your wife, and seeing you in my dreams, I continued the love that

---

[77] Honam is the southwestern portion of the Korean peninsula.

[78] The text indicates that she studied the *kŏmun'go* and *sŏ* (letters), which would include writing, poetry, calligraphy, and reading.

> I will never forget. I was too sad to listen to the song of the cuckoo in the pear tree or the sound of the night rain on the leaves of the paulownia tree. I could not even gaze at the trails of the fireflies outside my window or the lonely shadow of the solitary lamp in my room. Sometimes I just sit absently by the folding screen, and at other times, I alone go out to the railing where I secretly appeal to the blue sky for relief from the pent-up bitterness that binds the blood in my breast. I do not know: is my love also thinking of me? If I suddenly die before seeing my dearest, even if the heavens and earth vanish, my deeply sorrowful heart will not disappear. Today, the women of both palaces have gathered to do laundry, and for that reason I could not stay long. As my tears on this letter have smeared the ink, my spirit has dissipated and my bowels are as if pierced. I prostrate myself in supplication to once again see my love.

The letter was of the sorrow of gazing upon the autumn scenery and of wholly yearning for my love as well.

That evening Charan and I went out first in the direction of the East Gate. Sook, while smiling, gave me a quatrain that she had written. It was all about mocking my mind. I received the poem, enduring my embarrassed heart,

> As a stream flows around the front of T'aeŭl Shrine,
> Clouds scatter at the heavenly alter, and the nine gates open.[79]
> One with a thin waist cannot overcome the violent gale,
> Momentarily hidden in the forest, but then returning
> with dusk.

Then Pigyŏng, Kŭmnyŏn, Puyong, and Poryŏn all gave a verse—they were all teasing me. Riding a horse, I came out first and went back to the shaman's house. The shaman, seeming quite indignant, sat facing the wall and did not turn around at my arrival. When I saw the *chinsa* upon my arrival, he had been wringing his hands and sobbing, his face covered with pearl-like teardrops. I took off a gold ring with a jade stone from my left hand and put it next to his chest, saying, "My dearest, since you did not consider me as unworthy, and brought your body—as precious as a thousand gold pieces—to wait for me in such a humble place as this, I truly thank you. Although I am not sagacious, I am neither wood nor stone. How, even at death, could I not venerate my dearest? If I ever go back on my words, this gold ring is a pledge of my sincerity."

[79] The nine gates seems to be an allusion to the royal palace.

Then, as a long trip awaited me, I rose to leave, whispering in his ear, "I am at the Western Palace; if you take advantage of nightfall and come over the western wall, our unfinished destiny from three lives can be complete."[80]

I finished speaking, brushed off my clothes, and went out. I arrived at the palace gate first, with the other eight arriving after me.

That night at the second watch,[81] Sook and Pigyŏng, lighting their way with a lamp, came to the Western Palace. Pigyŏng said, "The poems written this afternoon seem to have conveyed unintentional jesting. Thus despite the deep night, we have come to apologize in utmost sincerity."

Hearing this, Charan said, "All of the five poems came from [those of] the Southern Palace. After we were divided into the Southern and Western palaces, the situation is very much like that of the Tang factional struggles led by Niu Seng-ru and Li Zong-min.[82] How can you say it is not due to suspicion? Nonetheless, as we know, women all have the same heart. For long, we have been confined to this secluded palace, consoled by only a solitary shadow, facing but the light of a lamp while playing the *kŏmun'go* and singing songs. The blossoms of a hundred flowers form and smile, and pairs of swallows fly about abreast. All we can do is gaze upon these things and feel sorrow, how else could such hearts be? The fairy of the morning clouds frequently visited the dreams of the King of Zhou,[83] Xiwang-mu joined many feasts on the Jeweled Terrace.[84] A woman's heart is no different from this. Why are we of the two palaces, alone together with Hanga,[85]

---

[80] The three lives (*samsaeng*) mentioned here are those of the past, present, and future.

[81] The second watch (*igyŏng*) is from 9 to 11 P.M.

[82] The text refers to the Niu-Li zhi-dang (factions of Niu and Li). Niu Seng-ru (779–847) was a minister in Tang China and in 823 colluded with Li Zong-min to purge an opponent and become prime minister. The faction headed by these two men was known as the Niu-Li faction and engaged in a political struggle that lasted some forty years.

[83] This is a reference to the aforementioned dream of Mt. Wu and is a metaphor for sexual union between a man and women.

[84] Xiwang-mu (the Queen Mother of the West) is a heavenly fairy mentioned earlier. The Jeweled Terrace is a house made of jade, or a magnificent palace.

[85] The text refers to Hanga (C. Henge), a fairy said to live on the moon. Her husband Ye received a magical elixir for immortality from Xiwang-mu. Hanga stole this elixir, became a fairy, and fled to the moon.

steadfastly keeping our anguish of fidelity and not repenting for the elixir we have stolen?"

Sook and Pigyŏng could not stop their tears: "The heart of one person is exactly the heart of all people. Receiving your excellent instruction, the sadness within us is blossoming like a cloud."

The two rose, gave a deep bow, and left. I looked at Charan, saying, "This evening I made a solemn pledge with Kim *chinsa;* if he doesn't come to see me tonight, he surely will come over the wall tomorrow. When he comes, how shall I show my hospitality?"

Charan replied, "With layers of silk curtains and many ply of cloud-motif folding screens, what could there be to worry about? Liquor plentiful as a river and meats piled up as a levee, what is the worry to serve? If he doesn't come, what can you do, but if he comes, why would it be difficult to treat him?"

That night, sure enough he did not come.

When the *chinsa* stealthily looked around the palace, the wall was so high and precipitous [it seemed] that he could not go over it without wings. Thus, he went back home, and sat mutely with a troubled expression on his face. Among his slaves was one named T'ŭk, who was famous for knowing every sort of trick and scheme. He looked at his master's face, kneeled before him, and said, "Master *chinsa* surely you are not long for this world!"

He then threw himself on the ground crying. The *chinsa* squatted down, took his wrist, and emptied everything that was in his heart. T'ŭk then said, "How could you not have told me this before? I will devise a suitable plan for this task."

Soon he fashioned a ladder, which was very light to carry and could be easily folded and unfolded. When folded, it was just as easy to handle as a folding screen; when unfolded, it was as long as five or six steps. T'ŭk, teaching him how to use it, said, "Use this ladder to go over the palace wall. Inside you can unfold it, and when you come back you can do the same."

The *chinsa* had T'ŭk try the ladder on the garden wall and it worked just as he said it would. The *chinsa* was very pleased. That night when he was about to go to the palace, T'ŭk produced from under his jacket some fur and leather bootees while telling him, "Without these, it will be difficult to get there safely."

When the *chinsa* put on the bootees and walked, his steps on the ground were like those of a bird, with no sound. Thus shod, he went over the wall and then lay down on the ground within a stand of bamboo. The moonlight was bright like the day, and inside the palace was quiet. After a while, someone came out from the inside of the palace and while walking about, recited poems in a small voice. The *chinsa* pushed aside the bamboo and showed his face saying, "Ah, my loved one!"

The other person while laughing answered, "Young sir, come out! Please come out!"

The *chinsa* briskly walked out and then bowed, saying, "A young man, as I, could not overcome my youthful passion, and risking ten thousand deaths dared to come. I pray that you, young maiden, do not fault me and place me somewhere safe."

Charan laughed, answering, "*Chinsa,* with your fine appearance that would easily move a heart, why would you cause me to have a life-long grudge against Unyŏng? We have waited for you to come like one would expect rain clouds during a severe drought. Fortunately I can now see you and we women can again live; I pray that you harbor no suspicions of me, sir."

She then guided the *chinsa* inside. I was sitting in my room alone with a gauze window open, a jade lamp brightly lit, a tulip-scented, animal-shaped golden fire pot, and a volume of *Taiping guangji* open on a glass desk in front of me.[86] When I saw him coming in, I rose to greet him and bowed, and he returned my bow and greeting. Like guest and master of the house, we separated and sat on the east and west. I had Charan prepare some delicacies and liquor, and together we drank cups of violet-colored liquor.[87] Then, somewhat drunkenly, he said, "How deep is the night?"

Charan understood his words and at once drew the curtains, closed the door, and went out. I put out the lamp and went to the sleeping mat with him; the pleasure of that night I cannot describe with words. The night soon turned to dawn; as the rooster urged the daybreak, the *chinsa* rose and went back. From that time on, there was not a night that he did not come at dusk and take leave at dawn. Our love became deeper and our affection for each other grew even warmer: we did not know how to stop these meetings. However, since there were traces of footprints in the snow around

---

[86] *Taiping guangji* [Extensive gleanings of the reign of Great Tranquility] is a massive compilation of legends and stories of the bizarre dating from the Han dynasty to the Five Kingdoms period (907–960) in China compiled in five hundred volumes by Li Fang in 983.

[87] The text refers to *chaha-ju,* which seems to be a refined liquor reserved for special occasions.

the palace walls, the palace people all considered this very dangerous.

One day, it suddenly came to the *chinsa* that all these pleasures would bring about a great calamity. He returned home and sat dejectedly and cheerlessly in an empty room. When my love was troubled as this, the servant T'ŭk returned from outside, saying, "Why have you not yet rewarded me for all my efforts?"

The *chinsa* said, "Your deed is engraved in my heart so I will not forget; sooner or later, of course I will generously reward you."

Then T'ŭk replied, "Now, looking at my master's face and color it seems that you are again worrying about something. What is it?"

The *chinsa* answered, "When I cannot see her, disease pierces my heart and the marrow of my bones; when I do see her, the crime for that cannot be even estimated. How can I not but worry?"

T'ŭk responded, "Then why don't you carry her off on your back unbeknownst to others and flee?"

The *chinsa* planned to do so, and that night he told me of T'ŭk's scheme. "Although T'ŭk is a slave, he has always been very resourceful. What do you think of this plan?"

I consented, saying, however, "My parents had a lot of property, and when I came here they sent along with me many clothes and treasures. Moreover, the Grand Prince has given me many things as well; I cannot abandon all these things and go. Now, if we want to move these things out, even ten horses could not carry it all. How should I take care of this?"

The *chinsa* returned home and talked to T'ŭk about this matter; the servant was very happy, saying, "Among my acquaintances, there are twenty with great strength. Nearly every day, they devote themselves to plundering, and not even government forces can easily match them. Since I am very close to them, they will follow my orders. If I have them transport it, even a great mountain could be moved. And if they guard the treasure, even ten thousand men could not easily steal it. Dismiss your myriad doubts, and let us settle on this plan early."

The *chinsa* came to the palace and told me this idea. I concurred, and every night we carried out the plan. After seven days, all the goods were moved outside the palace walls. T'ŭk said, "If such a treasure is piled up in your esteemed home, the elder lady will no doubt be suspicious.[88] If we pile it in my house, my

[88] The "elder lady" mentioned here could be the mother of Kim *chinsa*.

neighbors will surely be wary. It would be best to dig a hole in the mountains, bury the goods, and closely guard it."

The *chinsa* replied, "If this were ever to be lost, you and I would be accused as thieves and face great difficulties. You must guard this carefully."

T'ŭk answered, "My scheme is quite profound, and I have many friends as I have told you; thus, there can be no difficulties whatsoever on this earth. Moreover, I have a long sword and will not leave [the site of the treasure] day or night; although my eyes are plucked out, this treasure cannot be snatched away. I beg you not to worry."

In fact, T'ŭk's intent was to get hold of the treasure and then lead us to a mountain valley where he would kill the *chinsa* and make the treasure and me his. The *chinsa* was but a naïve scholar, and had no inkling of this scheme.

At this time, the Grand Prince wanted to have a beautiful poem to hang as a signboard at Pihae-dang, which had been built earlier. As he had not been satisfied with the poems of several literary men, he invited the *chinsa,* asked him to compose a poem, and offered a feast in solicitation. The *chinsa* whirled about the writing brush and composed one; it was so well written that not even a single word more was needed. There was nothing not expressed about the landscapes of mountains and streams as well as Pihae-dang itself in the poem. This poem was so well written that it would surprise even the wind and rain, and cause a ghost to wail. The Grand Prince, praising every word he read, said, "Unexpectedly, today again I see Wang Bo!"

The Grand Prince did not stop reciting the poem. However, coming upon the line "following the wall and quietly stealing romance," he stopped reciting and became suspicious of the *chinsa.* The *chinsa* rose and bowed, saying, "I am drunk and have lost my senses! I beg my lord to retire."

The Grand Prince ordered a manservant to assist him and sent him off.

The next night, the *chinsa* came to me and said, "It would be best to flee. After reading the poem I composed yesterday, the Grand Prince is now suspicious of me. I fear there will be future trouble unless we take flight tonight."

I replied, "In my dream last night I saw a person whose appearance was ferocious. He claimed to be Modon, the chieftain of the Huns,[89] and told me, 'Since there is a long-standing pledge,

[89] Modon was a chieftain (*tanu*) of the Huns during the Former Han dynasty.

I have waited for long under a long castle wall.' I awoke with surprise. Such a portentous dream does not bode well. What do you think of this?"

The *chinsa* replied, "Dreams have many falsities, so how can you believe it?"

I said, "The long wall he spoke of was the castle wall, and Modon is T'ŭk. My dearest, how well do you know the heart of that slave?"

"That slave is originally a wicked lowlife. However, the tie I have today together with you my dear is all the result of his schemes. Why would he first be loyal and then do an evil thing in the end?"

I answered, "My dearest, how can I not follow what you say? However, I share a deep bond with Charan like a sister; I must tell her about my departure."

Then I called Charan and as the three of us sat facing one another, I informed her of the plan. She was greatly surprised and scolded me: "Do you intend to bring about calamity for you both because you have been enjoying each other for too many days? It should have been sufficient for you two to be close for a month or two, but how could you even consider scaling the wall and fleeing? The first reason you cannot flee is that the Grand Prince has long been inclined toward you; the second reason is that the wife of the Grand Prince has been exceedingly concerned about you and loved you; the third reason is because the calamity would reach both of your families; and the fourth reason you should not run away is the blame that would fall upon the Western Palace. Heaven and the earth are no more than the same net, unless you go up to the heavens or under the ground, where could you possibly go although you run away? Moreover, if you are caught, do you think the suffering would stop only at you? The inauspicious omen in your dream need not be mentioned. Yet if your dream had been propitious, would you joyfully leave? What you should do is grasp hold of your mind and suppress your urgent heart, maintain your fidelity and while peacefully sitting, listen only to heaven's words. When you gradually grow older, the favor and love of the Grand Prince will likewise recede. In a situation that you were for long lying in bed under the

---

He reigned 209–174 BCE and was able to conquer various peoples in central Asia and bring the Huns to their zenith of power, eventually defeating the Han on the battlefield and extracting tribute from the Chinese state thereafter.

pretext of illness, the Grand Prince would undoubtedly allow you to return to your home. When that time comes, you can leave here with the *chinsa* hand in hand and live happily ever after. There is no plan better than this. Not even trying to think of a way like this, you dare to raise an unreasonable scheme. Whom do you think you can deceive, and moreover, do you hope to deceive the Grand Prince?"

At that, the *chinsa* knew that he would not be able to realize his plan and with tears in his eyes went out.

One day the Grand Prince was sitting under an embroidered silken tent at the Western Palace and saw a royal azalea in full bloom. He ordered us palace women of the Western Palace to each compose a verse [regarding the flower]. We composed our verses and presented them to the Grand Prince; he looked over our efforts, highly praising us.

"I am very pleased to see you all gradually, day by day, improve your writing. However, in Unyŏng's poems I can see her heart yearning for a lover. I could dimly sense such a feeling from the poem you wrote about the smoke. Now again, who is this person you want to go after? The other day when Scholar Kim wrote a poem there was a suspicious part as well; is it not Scholar Kim that you are thinking of?"

On hearing this I instantly fell down, putting my head on the ground and crying, "Earlier when I first incurred the suspicion of my Lord, I intended to kill myself. However, as I am not yet twenty and if I were to die without seeing my parents again it would be very regrettable, I have preserved my life and lived until this moment. Now again I am the object of your suspicions; how can I consider it lamentable for my life to end? While all the ghosts of heaven and earth were illuminating all around me, and despite the ten of us palace women having not been separated for a moment, a dirty name is given to me alone. To live now is not any better than to die. I have finally received a time to die."

At once, I took a silk scarf and tied it around my neck and to the railing. Then Charan spoke.

"While the Grand Prince is perspicacious, he still sends a guiltless palace maid to the jaws of death. From here forward, I swear an oath never to pick up a brush and write with it."

Even if the Grand Prince was very angry, in his heart he did not truly want me to die. Thus, he had Charan save me and allowed me to live. He then bestowed five bolts of silk cloth upon us, saying, "I give this as a prize to the five of you since the poems you composed were most beautiful."

After this, the *chinsa* could not come into the palace again and confined himself to his home, lying sick in bed. His tears drenched his blanket and pillow, and his life hung by a thin thread. T'ŭk saw him and said, "A brave man should die as worthy of such a name. How can you languish in heartbreak, yearning for your lover like a petty woman and seek to throw away your body as precious as a thousand gold pieces? Now, I request that you hear my polished plan, and it will not be difficult at all to get that woman. On a deep and tranquil night, if I climb over the wall, cover her mouth with cotton, and carry her on my back and run, who would dare stop or chase after us?"

The *chinsa* replied, "Your scheme is quite dangerous; I would rather go and ask her with a sincere heart."

That night the *chinsa,* came but since I was ill, I could not get up and instead had Charan greet him. After he was served three cups of wine, I gave him a sealed letter, telling him, "Since I won't be able to see you anymore after this, it seems the destiny of the three lives and our pledge of one hundred years is finished tonight. If the providence of the heavens is not severed, perchance we will find each other in the netherworld."

The *chinsa* took the letter and blankly stood looking at me. Then striking his breast and with tears flowing he went out. Charan, feeling pity for us, could not bear to look at us and leaned against a pillar while hiding her body, raining tears. The *chinsa* returned to his house and opened the letter, which read,

> The ill-fated woman Unyŏng bows to her dear lord and informs him the following. I, an unworthy character, unfortunately received your love. Since then, how long have we been longing for and missing each other? Fortunately, we were able to share nights of pleasure together, but we still did not exhaust our destiny of being together for three lives. The creatures of the universe are suspicious of all the good things of people, and as now the palace people know and the Grand Prince has become suspicious, calamity has drawn near. Only after I die will such calamity stop. I beg you my dearest, after I take leave of you, do not hold me in your heart with worries. Rather, study even more diligently. After you enter the path to high officialdom, be known by an honorable name by future generations and honor your parents. Sell my clothes and valuables and offer all to Buddha. Please pray for us in every way with all of your true heart so that our incomplete fate in this world can be completed in the next world. Good fortune! Good fortune!

The *chinsa* could not even finish reading the whole letter and fell into a faint. Those in his house quickly came to his aid, and he was revived. At that time, T'ŭk came in from outside: "With what kind of words did the palace lady answer that you intend to die like this?"

The *chinsa* had nothing more to say than "Have you been taking care of the valuables? I will carry out our old pledge by selling all the goods and offering the proceeds to Buddha."

T'ŭk went to his home alone, and thought to himself, "If the palace woman cannot come out [of the palace], the treasure is given to me by heaven."

He then secretly laughed toward the wall, but no one knew the reason. One day thereafter, he tore his clothes, struck his nose so blood flowed, dirtied his whole body, shook his hair loose, and then ran barefooted to the garden, where he threw himself on the ground, crying, "I've been robbed!"

He said no more, but acted as if he had fainted. The *chinsa* worried that if T'ŭk died he would not know the burial place of the treasure. So he poured medicinal water into T'ŭk's mouth and tried to revive him in every sort of way, even serving the slave liquor and meats. Finally, T'ŭk rose after ten days, explaining, "All alone in the mountains I was keeping watch [over the treasure] when there appeared a band of thieves who attacked me. As the situation was critical and life threatening, I ran away to save my life and barely escaped death. If it weren't for that treasure, why would my life have been in such danger? With such a harsh destiny, why hasn't this body died quickly?"

Then he stomped his feet on the ground, beat his chest, and wailed loudly. The *chinsa* feared that his parents would hear this and thus solaced him before sending him off.

Some days later, the *chinsa* became aware of T'ŭk's true act and with some ten servants headed for his house, abruptly surrounding it before having the servants search the place. However, they found nothing except a pair of golden hairpins and a jeweled mirror. He wanted to present these articles as proof of the theft at a government office and then find all the rest by making a criminal complaint against T'ŭk, but he feared that the entire matter would be revealed. Also, without treasure he could not offer the proceeds to Buddha, and although in his mind he wanted to kill T'ŭk, he could not easily defeat him by force. Thus, he had no choice but to keep his mouth closed.

T'ŭk, on his own accord, realized his crime and went to see a blind fortune-teller outside the palace walls.

"The other day at dawn I passed by the castle wall, and someone came out climbing over the palace wall. I was sure that he was a thief and while yelling loudly, I gave chase to him. The thief threw down the items he was carrying and scurried off. I took the stuff and returned home, concealing the property and waiting for its owner to come looking for it. However, my master, who has a character that knows no shame, heard that I had come upon some valuables and came to my house seeking the goods. I told him that there was no treasure except a hairpin and a mirror. Although he himself came looking for the treasure and indeed found only these, he was not satisfied and now wants to kill me. So I wish to flee; if I do so, will I be safe?"

The blind fortune-teller answered, "Yes, you will be safe."

A person standing to the side heard all of this and looked at T'ŭk, saying, "What kind of master do you have that would mistreat a servant like that?"

T'ŭk replied, "Although my master is young, he is skilled at letters and will undoubtedly soon pass the government service examination. However, his greed reaches to the same heights, and it is thus not difficult to predict his future malice when he becomes a government official."

This story spread and reached the palace, where the palace attendants informed the Grand Prince, who became greatly angered and had those of the Southern Palace go to the Western Palace and search for the clothing and treasure. There were none of my clothes or treasure to be found. The Grand Prince summoned the five of us from the Western Palace to the middle of the courtyard. There were clubs for beating criminals before our eyes, as we heard the order of the Grand Prince: "Kill these five and discipline the others!" Then he ordered the executioners who were holding the clubs, "Beat them regardless of the number of strokes until they die!"

At this, the five of us began to appeal: "We beg of you, let us speak once before killing us!"

The Grand Prince responded, "Whatever it was, tell everything that has happened."

First Ŭnsŏm gave her petition: "The desire between men and women is endowed by yin and yang, and as all humans possess this quality it does not distinguish whether one is noble or base. Once confined to this vast palace, our shadows were our companions as we passed time in loneliness. Tears cloud our eyes even when looking at flowers, and our spirits are depressed when confronted with the moon. It is for no other reason that we cast apricots at orioles so that they cannot fly in pairs and put beaded screens between swallows to prevent them from building a single nest. It is all because we could not bear our own jealous hearts that we envy pairs of orioles and swallows flying about. If we were to go over the palace wall, we could know the pleasures of the human world. That being so, we did not go over the palace wall because we lacked sufficient strength or because we did not have [such longings]. Only our fear of the Grand Prince has firmly kept our minds here as we wither away toward death. Yet, now, you intend to send us to our deaths despite our being crimeless. Even if we die and wander about the depths of the next world, our eyes will not close [i.e., we will not rest]."

Next, Pich'wi gave her petition: "The love and favor of the Grand Prince is higher than a mountain and deeper than the sea. As we are deeply thankful but fearful, all we have done was no more than to devote ourselves to letters and music. Now an indelible dishonor has reached the Western Palace, and death is preferable to life. Now, prostrated on the ground in supplication, I beg to die quickly."

Third was Ongnyŏ, who appealed, "As I have been part of the glory of the Western Palace, how can I be exempted from the misfortune of the Western Palace? When there was a fire on Mt. Kungang,[90] jade and rocks were both burnt;[91] as for today's death, I die but not from guilt."

Next, Charan offered her petition: "As we are all lowly women of the base class, we do not have for a father King Shun or for a mother one of his two queens.[92] How, then, would the passion between a man and woman be absent only in us? King Mu was a son of heaven, but nonetheless always recalled the pleasure of the jeweled terrace, and a hero like Xiang Yu could not hold back his tears at Gaixia.[93] How can the Grand Prince hold that Unyŏng

[90] Kungang is a reference to Mt. Kunlun, in Tibet. This mountain is said to have many beautiful stones such as jade.

[91] That is, both good and bad people suffer from calamity.

[92] King Shun is a legendary sage king of ancient China. The two empresses are the two wives of King Shun, Ehuang and Nuying, both of whom were the daughters of another sage king, Yao, the predecessor of Shun. Upon their husband's death, both of his queens are said to have jumped to their deaths in the Xiang River.

[93] King Mu, a king of Zhou, met Xiwang-mu (the Queen Mother of the West), an

alone does not have the desire of clouds and rain? Among men, Scholar Kim is the most handsome, and among the palace women, Unyŏng is one with deep bitterness in her heart. The one who brought him into the inner rooms was the Grand Prince, and the one who ordered Unyŏng to hold the inkstone for him was also my Lord. Unyŏng, a young woman with deep bitterness in her heart, upon seeing such a gallant man, lost her spirit and became mad with an illness that pierced the marrow of her bones. Even wondrous elixirs and the efficacy of Yue Ren's skills would not be any remedy for her.[94] If she is not killed by the cudgels now, her life will end by illness; thus, [even if you do] not order her killed, it will be her death nonetheless. I prostrate myself before the Grand Prince for you to be humane. Although foolish, I dare to think that there would be no more virtuous deed than if you, my Lord, would allow scholar Kim to meet Unyŏng and relieve their bitterness. The sin of Unyŏng's infidelity of the past days is not hers, but rather mine. Since I have endeavored not to deceive the desolate Grand Prince on one hand and have not discarded my comrades on the other, the death I am facing today will be honorable. I prostrate myself in front of my Lord and beg, please continue Unyŏng's life through my body."

Last of all, I petitioned: "The grace of the Grand Prince is like a mountain and the oceans. Despite that, not maintaining my fidelity is my first crime. My second crime is the poem I wrote on an earlier day that caused my Lord to become suspicious of me. And my third crime is that the guiltless women of the Western Palace are being punished on my behalf. With crimes such as these, with what countenance can I possibly live? Although you might delay my death, it is most suitable that I kill myself."

The Grand Prince finished looking at these petitions and then again unfolded the one written by Charan, and gradually his

---

aforementioned heavenly fairy who assisted the rulers of ancient China, on the jeweled terrace and could never forget the pleasure that they shared.

Xiang Yu (232–202 BCE) was a warlord of the late Chu kingdom. In 209 BCE he attacked the Qin kingdom (221–207 BCE) and destroyed it, thus becoming king of Western Chu. Subsequently, he was not able to reach a peace accord with Liu Bang (the personal name of Gaozu [247?–195 BCE], the founder of the Former Han dynasty) and was defeated in battle at Gaixia and forced to commit suicide.

At the battle of Gaixia, Xiang Yu's camp was encircled by Han troops. Together with his favorite mistress, he sang the "Song of Gaixia" with flowing tears before committing suicide.

[94] The reference is to the medicine of immortality (*changsaeng chi yak*). Yue Ren was a renowned medical man of the Warring States period in China.

anger seemed to subside. At that moment, Sook, who was kneeling, cried in appeal, "When we were to go and do laundry, I was of the opinion that we should not go inside the castle gates. Charan came to the Southern Palace at night and very earnestly appealed to us, and as I thought her heart pitiful, I rejected the others' opinions and followed her idea. Thus, the crime of Unyŏng's infidelity is mine and not hers. I implore my Lord to let Unyŏng live through my body!"

At that, the Grand Prince became somewhat less angry. He had me confined in a separate room and had all the other palace women released [to their quarters]. That night, I used a silken scarf to hang myself and died.

The *chinsa* had been writing the words in which Unyŏng recollected the past events, capturing every detail. The two looked at each other, unable to hold back the flood of sorrow. A while later, Unyŏng looked at the *chinsa*, saying, "From here, my dearest should tell the story."

The *chinsa* then continued Unyŏng's story.

After Unyŏng committed suicide, all of the palace people lamented as if their own mother had died. The sounds of mourning could be heard outside the place gates, and I also heard this, fainting for a long spell. The people of my house prepared rites to solace the spirit of the dead and announced my death, while at the same time trying with all their efforts to revive me. Only after the day had grown dark were they barely able to rouse me. However, I could not renege on my oath to make offerings to the Buddha. To solace her spirit, I sold Unyŏng's remaining gold hairpins and mirror and all of my writing implements, and prepared forty sacks of rice with the money.[95] I intended to send it to Ch'ŏngnyŏng Temple, where it could be offered to the Buddha. However, since there was no servant I could trust, I summoned T'ŭk, asking him, "If I forgive all of your previous crimes, will you now pledge loyalty to me?"

T'ŭk prostrated himself on the ground, and while crying said, "Even though I am ignorant of principles and dimwitted, I am neither wood nor stone. I have committed innumerable sins, so many so that they would be hard to count even if I pulled out all my hair as a measure. However, you have generously forgiven

[95] Forty *sŏk*. A *sŏk* is a measure of grain equivalent to roughly 5.12 US bushels.

me, which is the same as a dead tree sprouting leaves or a skeleton regaining its flesh. How can I even hesitate in devoting my life to you now?"

I responded, "For Unyŏng I wish to prepare an offering to the Buddha, but there is none whom I can trust. Will you go [on my behalf]?"

T'ŭk replied, "I humbly accept the bidding of my master."

T'ŭk left right away for the temple. After three days of lying down in a room and massaging his backside, he called to a monk and said, "How can you use all forty sacks of this rice in offerings to the Buddha? Rather, it would be best if you were to prepare a feast of liquor and foods and send out an invitation to monks and laymen near and far."

At that time, a village woman was passing by. T'ŭk violated her by force, taking her into the monastery and keeping her there. After some tens of days had passed but there seemed no sign of a Buddhist service for the deceased, all the monks of the temple became quite indignant. On the day to offer the rites to Buddha, a monk said to T'ŭk, "In offering a Buddhist service, the benefactor is very important. Since you the benefactor are unclean as this, it is not appropriate for a proper offering to the Buddha. We suggest that it would be good to carry out this rite after you wash yourself in a clear stream and make your body clean."

T'ŭk had no choice but to go out, hastily wash, and then return, kneeling before the Buddha and praying, "Please let the *chinsa* die quickly today and Unyŏng live again tomorrow and become mine."

Like this, for three days and nights, he prayed, saying no words other than these. When he returned, he told me, "The young lady Unyŏng will undoubtedly live again. On the night of the day that the rites were offered, there appeared in my dream a pretty young woman with a silk scarf tied around her neck. She said to me, 'You are my small master and I am your woman Unyŏng. As the sincere heart and effort you devoted for me are truly large and wide, even the Buddha would not have any other choice but to be deeply touched. I will surely and generously reward you.' Moreover, all the monks at the temple also had a same dream."

Believing his words, I told him, "Now, on my behalf you have acted sincerely; for the first time I realize your loyalty," and then wailed in grief.

Finally, it was the season when the cassia tree leaves turned yellow.[96] Even though I had no thought of sitting for the examinations, under the pretext of study I went up to Ch'ŏngnyŏng Temple. I stayed for a few days and heard in detail what T'ŭk had done; I could not overcome my rage. However, it was not as if I could do something to T'ŭk. I bathed and cleansed myself and then went before the Buddha, lowering my body to bow one hundred times. Lowering my head and lighting incense, I put my hands together and prayed.

"The words of Unyŏng at her death—such misery I cannot endure. I ordered my slave T'ŭk to sincerely offer rites for her happiness in the next life, yet today I heard of the prayers of T'ŭk and his indescribable wickedness. Now Unyŏng's dying wishes have futilely vanished. For me, I only desire a quick death, but still, how can I not be enraged? This small person dares again to pray to you. Prostrate before you I beg, oh Buddha! Let Unyŏng live again and be my wife, and allow us to live together for ten thousand years. Oh Buddha! I beg that you allow Unyŏng to reach the next world and be my wife and resume our incomplete destiny. Oh Buddha! I beg that you kill the slave T'ŭk, put a sword in him and confine him to the underworld. Oh Buddha! Prostrated before you I beg that you kill the slave T'ŭk, boil him hard and throw [the remains] to the starving hounds. Oh Buddha! Prostrated before you I beg that if you only do such, Unyŏng will build a twelve-story gold pagoda, and I will build three great villages and six temples to repay your great grace."

I prayed while making one hundred deep bows, touching my head to the floor, and then left.

After seven days, T'ŭk fell into a pit [and died].[97] The corpse was abandoned along the road, and sure enough his body was torn apart and eaten by hungry dogs. From this time, I had no interest in worldly matters. I bathed to make my body pure, dressed in new clothes, and lay down in a quiet room. I did not eat for four days, and finally, I deeply sighed once more and never again rose.

---

[96] That is, the time for the autumn government service examinations (*kwagŏ*) held in the seventh lunar month.

[97] The text informs us that he fell into a *hamjŏng,* a type of pit dug to capture animals.

After finishing writing, the two looked at each other and could not control their sadness. Scholar Yu, consoling the two, said, "As the wish you had to meet again has come true and also as your foe the slave has been eliminated, your fury is somewhat washed away. Why do you not check your anger and sorrow? Are you grieving for not being born again in the human world?"

With tears flowing, Scholar Kim gratefully replied, "We both died with bitterness in our hearts. Myŏngsa considered us who had died without crime as pitiful, and intended to have us reborn in the human world again.[98] However, the pleasures of the underworld are not less than those of the human world, and the pleasures of the heavens are greater. For this reason, we did not desire to come back to the human world. Only, on this evening are we feeling sorrow to see the old palace without its master, and only crows and swallows sadly singing. Over yonder, after the fires from the war, the magnificent homes are in ashes, and the whitewashed walls are in ruined heaps. All that remain are the fragrance of the flowers near the stone steps and the lush grasses in the yard. Spring light does not change the scenes of yore, yet matters of the human world have changed to this. We came to this place to reminisce about long ago. How can we not be sad?"

Yu Yŏng asked, "Then the two of you became heavenly beings?"

Kim answered, "Originally, we were heavenly fairies and for long served the Jade Emperor. One day the emperor came to T'aech'ŏng Palace and ordered me to bring some fruit plucked from the Jade Garden.[99] At that time, Unyŏng and a group of fairies were playing at Mt. Oktong. I tossed in jest to Unyŏng many of the *pando* peaches[100] and jewels that I gathered, and she also threw to me the fruit of a golden lotus. The Jade Emperor saw these transgressions, and for this crime, the two of us were sent to the human world at the same time and forced to undergo the sufferings of the carnal world. Now the Jade Emperor has pardoned our earlier transgression and allowed us to again go up to Samch'ŏng Palace to serve before the incense table. We received an order to rest and rode a chariot about, again coming down from the heavens to this world, and seeking the old spots where we used to frolic about."

---

[98] Myŏngsa is the administrator of the next world.

[99] The Jade Garden is a beautiful garden preserve in the heavenly world.

[100] *Pando* peaches are fruit of immortality.

With tears flowing, Kim held Unyŏng's hands and continued, "Although the seas have dried up and rocks have crumbled to nothingness, and even if the earth is aged and the heavens tumble, our bitterness will not be appeased. Tonight, meeting with you, sir, we have been able to speak frankly and truthfully of what is in our minds: if not for the destiny of a previous life, how else would this be possible? Dear sir, please take this writing and pass it on to the world for the ages. Moreover, please keep this from frivolous people who speak indiscriminately and take it as trifling. All I wish is that you do such."

Kim *chinsa* drunkenly leaned on Unyŏng and recited one verse of poetry:

Within the palace [covered] by fallen flowers, swallows
  and sparrows fly,
The spring light is still the same, but the master is no more.
The moonlight in the night sky is cool as this,
Small dewdrops lightly fall on my jade-green robe.

Unyŏng then recited her verse:

The flowers and willows in the old palace are girded
  with new spring light,
The splendid olden days of a thousand seasons past
  appear again and again in my dreams.
This evening we come here to seek traces of yore,
Unaware of bead-like tears drenching my handkerchief.

Unyŏng, with a loving countenance and heavenly voice said, "We must now together return the nine thousand leagues to the Jade Palace. The stars are fluttering and the moon is inclining as the night is quite deep; if we hurriedly flash the whip and return, we can arrive before the heavenly emperor by daybreak."

The *chinsa* responded, "We must now rise and take leave. Our words have embraced countless measures of grief, and these cannot be expunged in a single night. I beg that you treasure these words."

Suddenly they were gone. Not again [did Yu] see them. All he saw were clouds and smoke covering the ground. In the dawn light, the vast expanse of the four quarters was absent of human voices, and the valley echoed only the mournful cries of birds. Sad and dejected, at a rock's edge, he feigned sleep and waited for the morning, only then returning from this faraway place.

Character Glossary

a 雅
akkong 樂工
akpu 樂附

becoming clouds, becoming rain (*wiun wiu*) 爲雲爲雨
Bing Ji 丙吉
Book of Changes (*Yŏkkyŏng*) 易經
Book of Rites (*Yegi*) 禮記
Book of Songs (*Sigyŏng*) 詩經

Ch'ae Chegong (1720–1779) 蔡濟恭
Ch'ae Su (1449–1515) 蔡壽
chaha-ju 紫霞酒
Changan Castle (Changan sŏng) 長安城
Changhŏn taewang 莊憲大王
Changle Palace 長樂
"Changmen fu" 長門賦
changsaeng chi yak 長生之藥
Changsin Palace (Changsin gung) 長信宮
Changsŏ-gak Library 藏書閣
Charan 紫鸞
Cheng Hao (1032–1085) 程顥
Cheng I (1033–1107) 程頤
Cheng-tang 盛唐
chikchehak 直提學
chinsa 進士
Chiphyŏn-jŏn 集賢殿
ch'irŏn chŏlgu 七言絶句
Cho Sŏnggi (1638–1689) 趙聖期
Ch'oe Hŭnghyo 崔興孝
chŏktong 笛童
Chŏng Inji (1396–1478) 鄭麟趾
Chŏng Tojŏn (1342–1398) 鄭道傳
chŏnmin 田民
Chongmyo 宗廟
chŏnsŏn 典膳
chŏnŭi 典衣
"Chosin" 調信
Chosŏn dynasty (1392–1910) 朝鮮
Chowŏn Hall 朝元
Chu kingdom 楚
Chu-tang 初唐
chungch'u 仲秋
chwa u 左右
Compilation of Royal Edicts (*Sugyo chimnok*) 受敎輯錄
Comprehensive Later National Code, Supplemented (*Taejŏn-hu sok-rok*) 大典後續錄
concubine 妾
Conduct of the Three Bonds with Illustrations (*Samgang haengsil-to*) 三綱行實圖

Diary of Prince Yŏnsan (*Yŏnsan-gun ilgi*) 燕山君日記
Diary of the Year Kyech'uk (*Kyech'uk ilgi*) 癸丑日記
Diary of the Year Pyŏngja (*Pyŏngja ilgi*) 丙子日記
Dongfang Shuo 東方朔
Dream of Nine Clouds (*Kuun-mong*) 九雲夢
dream record (*mongyu-rok*) 夢遊錄
Dream Record of Master Wŏn (*Wŏn saeng mongyu-rok*) 元生夢遊錄
Dream Record of Susŏng Palace (*Susŏng-gung mongyu-rok*) 壽聖宮夢遊錄
Dream of the Jade Pavilion (*Ongnu-rok*) 玉樓夢
Du Fu (712–770; K. Tu Po) 杜甫

Ehuang 娥皇
Elementary Learning (*Sohak*) 小學
Elementary Matters of Etiquette for Scholar Families (*Sasojŏl*) 士小節
Emperor Wen (r. 180–157 BCE) 文帝
Emperor Wu 漢武帝
Emperor Xuan (r. 74–49 BCE) 宣帝
Emperor Xuanzong (r. 712–756) 玄宗
Empress Chen 陳皇后
Essentials of Koryŏ History (*Koryŏsa chŏryo*) 高麗史節要
eunuchs (*hwan'gwan*) 宦官
Expanded Conduct of the Three Bonds with Illustrations (*Sok samgang haengsil-to*) 續三綱行實圖
Extensive Gleanings of the Reign of Great Tranquility (*T'aep'yŏng gwang-gi*) 太平廣記

Faction of the meritorious and conservative (Hun'gu p'a) 勳舊派
fairy on Mt. Wushan (*Musan sŏnnyŏ*) 巫山仙女
Festival of the Eight Vows (P'algwan-hoe) 八關會
fidelity (*chŏngjŏl*) 貞節
five relationships (*oryun*) 五倫
following the wall and quietly stealing romance (*su jang am chŏl p'ung ryu kok*) 隨墻暗竊風流曲
Former Han dynasty 前漢
The Four Books for Women (*Yŏsasŏ*) 女四書
freeborn commoners (*yanga*) 良家
"Fu Changyang" 賦長楊

Gaixia 垓下
Gaozu (247?–195 BCE) 高祖
Grand Prince Anp'yŏng (1418–1453) 安平大君
Grand Prince Suyang (1417–1468) 首陽大君

ha mu wŏl ha yŏn 何無月下緣
Haedong kangsŏ 海東江西
hamjŏng 陷穽
han 恨
Hanga 姮娥
hansi 漢詩
Hanyang 漢陽
happon 合本
The History of the Koryŏ Dynasty (*Koryŏsa*) 高麗史
Hŏ Nansŏrhŏn (1562–1590) 許蘭雪軒
hojŏp-mong 蝴蝶夢
Honam 湖南
Huanghe River 黃河

Hŭigyŏng 義經
Hŭng 興
Hwangbo In (?–1453) 皇甫仁

igyŏng 二更
Im Che (1549–1587) 林悌
Im Yunjidang (1721–1793) 任允摯堂
inside people, i.e., women (*naein*) 內人
Instructions for the Inner Quarters (*Naehun*) 內訓
Inwang-san 仁王山
Inwang-san 仁旺山

The Jade Garden (Ogwŏn) 玉園
jeweled terrace (*yodae*) 瑤臺

kaa 歌兒
kaeguk kongsin 開國功臣
Kija 箕子
Kim Chongsŏ (1390–1453) 金宗瑞
Kim Manjung (1637–1692) 金萬重
Kim Sisŭp (1435–1493) 金時習
King Ch'unghye (r. 1330–1332; 1339–1344) 忠惠王
King Ch'ungnyŏl (r. 1274–1308) 忠烈王
King Hyojong (r. 1649–1659) 孝宗
King Kojong (r. 1864–1907) 高宗
King Kongmin (r. 1351–1374) 恭愍王
King Ling 靈王
King Mu 穆王
King Munjong (r. 1450–1452) 文宗
King Sejo (r. 1455–1468) 世祖
King Sejong (r. 1418–1450) 世宗
King Shun 舜
King Sŏngjong (r. 1469–1494) 成宗
King Sukchong (r. 1674–1720) 肅宗
King T'aejo (r. 1392–1398) 太祖
King Tanjong (r. 1452–1455) 端宗
King Yao 堯
King Yŏngjo (r. 1724–1776) 英祖
kisaeng 妓生
koksin 穀神
Koryŏ dynasty (918–1392) 高麗
Kŭmnyŏn 金蓮
Kungang 崑崗
kungwŏn si 宮怨詩
kunsu 郡守
kwagŏ 科擧
kwallye 冠禮
Kwanghae-gun (r. 1608–1623) 光海君
Kwŏn P'il (1569–1612) 權韠
Kwŏn Sŏkchuje 權石洲製
Kyŏngbok Palace 景福宮
kyŏnggae yakku 傾盖若舊
kyŏngnu 更漏
Kyŏnu-Chignyŏ sŏlhwa 牽牛織女說話

Lady Cho of Namp'yŏng (1574–1645) 南平曺氏
Lady Hong of Hyegyŏng Palace (1734–1815) 惠慶宮洪氏
Lady Kwikkuk (C. Lady Guoguo) 虢國夫人
Lao Zhao-rin (637–689?) 盧照鄰
Laozi 老子
Latter Han dynasty 後漢
li 里
Li Bai (701–762) 李白
Li Fang 李昉
Li Shang-yin (813–858) 李商隱
Li Yi-shan 李義山
Li Zong-min 李宗閔
literati purges (*sahwa*) 士禍

Liu Bang 劉邦
Luo Bin-wang (650–684) 駱賓王

Maengsi-dan 盟詩檀
Man is heaven (*pu nae ch'ŏn*) 夫乃天
manryŏk sinch'uk samwŏl kimang 萬曆辛丑三月既望
Master Kuang 師廣
Man-tang 晚唐
Memorabilia of the Three Kingdoms (*Samguk yusa*) 三國遺事
Men are exalted, women lowly (*namjon yobi*) 男尊女卑
Meng Hao-ran (689–740) 孟浩然
Miluoshui River 汨羅水
Miscellany by Yongjae (*Yongjae ch'onghwa*) 慵齋叢話
Modon 冒頓
Mt. Black Horse 驪山
Mt. Kunlun (K. Kollyun-san) 崑崙山
Mt. Mu (C. Wushan) 巫山
munmuk 文墨
munyŏ 巫女
Myŏngsa 冥司

naemyŏngbu 內命婦
National Code (*Kyŏngguk taejŏn*) 經國大典
New Tales of Mt. Golden Turtle (*Kŭmo sinhwa*) 金鰲新話
Niu Seng-ru (779–847) 牛僧孺
Niu-Li zhi-dang 牛李之黨
novels of the women's quarters (*kyubang sosŏl*) 閨房小說
Nuying 女英

Office of Royal Decrees (Yemun'gwan) 藝文館
Office of the Inspector-General (Sahŏn-bu) 司憲府

ogaek 玉液
Okch'ŏng 玉清
Ongnyŏ 玉女
ŏnmun 諺文
oŏn-si 五言詩

"Paeksŏl-gok" (C. Baixue-qu) 白雪曲
palace supply office (*naesusa*) 內需司
palace woman (*kungnyŏ*) 宮女
pando peaches (*pando*) 蟠桃
panggak-bon 坊刻本
pentasyllabic quatrain (*oŏn chŏlgu*) 五言絕句
pi 比
Pich'wi 翡翠
Pihae-dang 匪懈堂
Piyŏng 飛瓊
the Pleasure of Clouds and Rain (*un u chi rak*) 雲雨之樂
pokto 複道
Polaris (Pukkŭk sŏng) 北極星
Poryŏn 寶蓮
Prince Yŏnsan 燕山君
pu 賦
pudŏk 婦德
p'ung 風
Purge of 1453 (Kyeyu chŏngnan) 癸酉靖難
pusil 副室
Puyong 芙蓉

Qin kingdom 秦
Qu Yuan (343?–277?) 屈原
Queen Sohye (1437–1504) 昭惠王后
Queen Yanggue (719–756) 楊貴妃

A Record of Lady Sa's Trip to the South (*Sassi namjŏnggi*) 謝氏南征記

"Record of Playing *chŏp'o* at Manbok Temple" (Manbok-sa chŏp'o-ki) 萬福寺樗蒲記
Record of Sorrowful Days (*Hanjung-rok*) 閑中錄
Records of the Historian (*Sagi*) 史記
rules of the inner and outer (*nae oe-pŏp*) 內外法

sadaebu 士大夫
sahwa 士禍
Sajik Altar 社稷
Samch'ŏng 三淸
samsaeng 三生
Sangch'ŏng 上淸
sanggung 尙宮
sarim faction (*sarim p'a*) 士林派
sasik 司飾
sayuksin 死六臣
Se Fu 嗇夫
sech'aekka 貰冊家
second state councilor (*chwaŭijŏng*) 左議政
serving women (*sinyŏ*) 侍女
Short Essays by Paegun (*Paegun sosŏl*) 白雲小說
sima 詩魔
Sima Qian (145?–86? BCE) 司馬遷
Sima Xiangru (179–117 BCE) 司馬相如
sinsa 神祀
sinsŏn 神仙
sŏ 書
so yŏja 少女子
soa 騷雅
Sogyŏksŏ-dong 昭格署洞
sŏin 庶人
sŏk 石
sŏndo 仙桃
song 頌
Song dynasty 宋
Sŏng Hyŏn (1439–1504) 成俔
"Song of Gaixia" 垓下歌
Sŏng Sammun (1418–1456) 成三問
Song-style poetry (*Song-si*) 宋詩
Sook 小玉
"Student Yi Peers over the Wall" (Yi saeng kyujang-jŏn) 李生窺牆傳
Su Jin (?–317 BCE) 蘇秦
Su Shi (1036–1101) 蘇軾
suguk 水國
sunsŏng 順成
Supplement to the National Code (*Sok taejŏn*) 續大典
Susŏng Palace 壽聖宮
Sutra of the Yellow Court (*Hwang-jŏng-gyŏng*) 黃庭經

T'aech'ŏng 太淸
Taemyŏng ch'ŏn'gye isipil-nyŏn 大明天啓二十一年
taesik 對食
T'aeŭl-sa 太乙祠
The Tale of Cho Ung (*Cho Ung-jŏn*) 趙雄傳
The Tale of Ch'unhyang (*Ch'un-hyang-jŏn*) 春香傳
The Tale of Hong Kiltong (*Hong Kiltong-jŏn*) 洪吉童傳
The Tale of Lady Pak (*Pakssi-jŏn*) 朴氏傳
The Tale of Master Chu (*Chu saeng-jŏn*) 周生傳
The Tale of the Person in Green (*Nogŭi in-jŏn*) 綠衣人傳
The Tale of Queen Inhyŏn (*Inhyŏn wanghu-jŏn*) 仁顯王后傳
The Tale of Sim Ch'ŏng (*Sim Ch'ŏng-jŏn*) 沈淸傳
The Tale of Sukhyang (*Sukhyang-jŏn*) 淑香傳

The Tale of Unyŏng (*Unyŏng-jŏn*) 雲英傳
The Tale of Wei Kyŏngch'ŏn (*Wei Kyŏngch'ŏn-jŏn*) 韋敬天傳
The Tale of Yu Yŏng (*Yu Yŏng-jŏn*) 柳泳傳
tales of wonder (*chŏn'gi sosŏl*) 傳奇小說
Tang dynasty 唐
Tang-style poetry (*Tang-si*) 唐詩
T'angch'un-dae 蕩春臺
tanu 單于
That Goodness Be Manifest and Righteousness Prized (*Ch'angsŏn kamŭi-rok*) 彰善感義錄
three bonds (*samgang*) 三綱
Three Kingdoms period (1st cent BCE–7th cent CE) (Samguk sidae) 三國時代
three obediences (*sam chong chi do*) 三從之道
t'osin 土神
tŭng yong mun 登龍門

u ch'o chi sim 憂楚之心
ŭmnyŏ 淫女
ŭmsa 淫祀
Ŭnsŏm 銀蟾
Unyŏng 雲英
unyu-ju 雲乳酒

Veritable Records of King Chungjong (*Chungjong sillok*) 中宗實錄
Veritable Records of King Hyojong (*Hyojong sillok*) 孝宗實錄
Veritable Records of King Sejong (*Sejong sillok*) 世宗實錄
Veritable Records of King Sŏngjong (*Sŏngjong sillok*) 成宗實錄
Veritable Records of King T'aejo (*T'aejo sillok*) 太祖實錄
Veritable Records of King Yŏngjo (*Yŏngjo sillok*) 英祖實錄

Wang Bo (650–676) 王勃
Wang Wei (699–759) 王維
Wang Yang-ming (K. Wang Yang-myŏng) 王陽明
Wang Zijin 王子晉
wansa 浣紗
Warring States period (475–221 BCE) (Chŏn'guk sidae) 戰國時代
Western Chu kingdom 西楚
Weiyang Palace 未央宮
Wenzong (r. 827–840) 文宗
Wŏlha noin 月下老人
a woman must follow her husband (*yŏ p'il chong pu*) 女必從夫
wŏnmang 遠望
"Writing of the Earthen Altar" (Pongsŏn mun) 封禪文
"Writing to Drive Away a Poetry Ghost" (Kusima mun) 驅詩魔文

Xiwang-mu 西王母
Xiang Yu (232–202 BCE) 項羽

yaje 野祭
yang (K. *yang*) 陽
Yang Jiong (650–700?) 楊炯
yangban 兩班
yangga 良家
Yi Kyojin 李僑鎭
Yi Kyubo (1168–1241) 李奎報
Yi Sŏnggye (1335–1408) 李成桂
yin (K. *ŭm*) 陰
yŏlli 連理
yŏngjwa 靈座
Yongmun (C. Longmen) 龍門

Yŏnyung-dae 鍊戎臺
yŏwŏn 女怨
yŏyŏm 閭閻
Yu Yŏng (1553–1616) 柳泳
Yuan Ji (210–263 CE) 阮籍
Yue Ren 越人
yuha-chu 流霞酒
Zhang Shi-zhi 張釋之
Zhong-tang 中唐
Zhou dynasty 周
Zhuangzi (365–290 BCE) 莊子
Zimei (K. Chami) 子美
Zhu Xi (1130–1200; K. Chu Hŭi) 朱熹

Bibliography

Primary Sources

Cho-ssi. *Pyŏngja ilgi* [丙子日記 Diary of the year *pyŏngja* {i.e., 1636}]. Translation and annotations Chŏn Hyŏngdae and Pak Kyŏngsin. Seoul: Yejŏnsa, 1991.

Chosŏn wangjo sillok [朝鮮王朝實錄 Veritable records of the Chosŏn dynasty]. Reproduction of original. Seoul: Kuksa pyŏnch'an wiwŏnhoe, 1955–1958.

Im, Che. *Wŏn-saeng mongnyu-rok* [元生夢遊錄 Dream record of Master Wŏn]. In *Han'guk ko sosŏl sŏn* [Compilation of classical Korean novels]. Seoul: T'aehaksa, 1995.

Iryŏn. *Samguk yusa* [三國遺事 Memorabilia of the Three Kingdoms]. Translation Yi Minsu. Seoul: Ŭryu munhwasa, 1994.

Kim, Sisŭp. *Kŭmo sinhwa* [金鰲新話 New tales of Mt. Golden Turtle]. Translation and annotations Sim Kyŏngho. Seoul: Hongik ch'ulp'ansa, 2000.

Koryŏsa [高麗史 The history of the Koryŏ dynasty]. Reproduction of original. Seoul: Asea munhwasa, 1990.

Koryŏsa chŏryo [高麗史節要 Essentials of Koryŏ history]. Reproduction of original. Seoul: Myŏngmundang, 1991

Kyŏngguk taejŏn [經國大典 National code]. Translation Yun Kugil. Seoul: Sin sŏwŏn, 1998.

Lizhi [禮記 Book of rites]. Translation Yi Minsu. Seoul: Hyewŏn ch'ulp'ansa, 1995.

Sijing [詩經 Book of poetry]. Translation Yi Sangjin et al. Seoul: Chayu mun'go, 1994.

Sok taejŏn [續大典 Supplement to the national code]. Seoul: Sŏul taehakkyo Kyujanggak, 1998.

Sŏng, Hyŏn. *Yŏngjae ch'onghwa* [慵齋叢話 Miscellany by Yŏngjae]. Reproduction of original. Seoul: Hangmin munhwasa, 2000.

Su, Shi. *Dongpo quanji* [東坡全集 The collected works of Dongpo]. Digital version.

Sugyo chimnok [受敎輯錄 Compilation of royal edicts]. Reproduction of original. Seoul: Pŏjech'ŏ, 1964.

Taejŏn sok-rok [大典續錄 Comprehensive national code, supplemented]. Reproduction of original. Seoul: Asea munhwasa, 1983.

Taejŏn-hu sok-rok [大典後續錄 Comprehensive later national code, supplemented]. Reproduction of original. Seoul: Asea munhwasa, 1983.

Unyŏng-jŏn [雲英傳 The tale of Unyŏng], Asami version.

Unyŏng-jŏn [雲英傳 The tale of Unyŏng], Changsŏgak version.

Yi, Kyubo. *Paegun sosŏl* [白雲小說 Short essays by Paegun]. In Hong Manjong, *Sihwa ch'ongnim* [詩話叢林 Comprehensive collection of essays on poetry]. Seoul: T'ongmun'gwan, 1993.

———. *Tongguk Yi Sangguk chip* [東國李相國集 Collected works of Minister Yi of the Eastern Country]. Reproduction of original. Seoul: Myŏngmundang, 1982.

Yi, Tŏkmu. *Sasojŏl* [士小節 Elementary matters of etiquette for scholar families]. Translation Kim Chonggwŏn. Seoul: Myŏngmundang, 1987.

Secondary Sources

Bakhtin, Mikhail. *The Dialogic Imagination.* Ed. Michael Holquist, trans. Caryl Emerson and Michael Holquist. Austin: University of Texas Press, 1981.

de Bary, Wm. Theodore, and Irene Bloom, eds. *Sources of Chinese Tradition,* 2nd ed. Vol. 1: *From Earliest Times to 1600.* New York: Columbia University Press, 1999.

Ch'a Sangwŏn and Chang Kigŭn. *Kosŏ myŏngŏn-myŏnggu sajŏn* [Dictionary of famous words and phrases in classical writings]. Seoul: P'yŏngbŏmsa, 1980.

Cho Hŭiung. *Kojŏn sosŏl ibon mongnok* [Catalog of alternative titles for classical novels]. Seoul: Chimmundang, 1999.

Cho Tongil. *Han'guk munhak t'ongsa* [A complete history of Korean literature]. 5 vols. Seoul: Chisik sanŏpsa, 1991.

Ch'oe Sukkyŏng and Ha Hyŏngang. *Han'guk yŏsŏng sa: Kodae Chosŏn sidae* [A history of Korean women: From ancient times through the Chosŏn period]. Seoul: Ihwa yŏja taehakkyo ch'ulp'anbu, 1993.

Ch'oe Honggi et al. *Chosŏn chŏn'gi kabuchangje wa yŏsŏng* [The patriarchal system and women in early Chosŏn]. Seoul: Ak'anet, 2004.

Ch'oe Hyejin. *Kyuhun munhak yŏn'gu* [A study of women's educational literature]. Seoul: Yŏngnak, 2004.

Ch'oe, Yongho; Peter H. Lee; and Wm. Theodore de Bary, eds. *Sources of Korean Tradition.* Vol. 2. New York: Columbia University Press, 2000.

Choe-Wall, Yang Hi. *Vision of a Phoenix: The Poems of Hŏ Nansŏrhŏn.* Cornell East Asia series, no. 117. Ithaca, N.Y.: East Asia Program, Cornell University, 2003.

Chŏn Wan'gil. *Han'guk ŭi yŏsok* [Women's lives in Korea]. Seoul: Usŏk ch'ulp'ansa, 1980.

Chŏn Yongmun. *Han'guk yŏsŏng yŏn'gung sosŏl ŭi yŏn'gu* [A study of Korean heroine novels]. Seoul: Mogwŏn taehakkyo ch'ulp'anbu, 1996.

Chŏng Chaesu. "*Yŏllyŏ-jŏn* ŭi yŏsŏng yuhyŏnghak" [Typology of women in the *Yŏllyŏ-jŏn*]. In *Tong Asia yŏsŏng ŭi kiwŏn:* Yŏllyŏ-jŏn-e *taehan yŏsŏnghakchŏk t'amgu* [The origins of East Asian women: A woman's study investigation concerning the *Yŏllyŏ-jŏn*], ed. Ihwa Chungguk yŏsŏng munhak yŏn'gu-hoe, 15–23. Seoul: Ihwa yŏja taehakkyo ch'ulp'anbu, 2002.

Chŏng Ch'anggwŏn. *Han'guk kojŏn yŏsŏng sosŏl ŭi chaebalgyŏn* [A rediscovery of classical Korean women's novels]. Seoul: Chisik sanŏpsa, 2002.

Chŏng Ch'urhŏn. *Kojŏn sosŏlsa ŭi kudu wa sigak* [Structure and view in classical novel history]. Seoul: Sop'yŏng ch'ulp'an, 1999.

Chŏng Ch'urhŏn et al. *Kojŏn munhak kwa yŏsŏngjuŭi-jŏk sigak* [Korean classical literature from a feminist perspective]. Seoul: Somyŏng ch'ulp'an, 2003.

Chŏng Haeŭn. "Ponggŏn ch'eje ŭi tongyo wa yŏsŏng ŭi sŏngjang" [Tremors in the structure of feudal society and the growth of women]. In *Uri yŏsŏng ŭi yŏksa* [The history of Korean women], ed. Han'guk yŏsŏng yŏn'guso, 225–250. Seoul: Ch'ŏngnyŏnsa, 1999.

Chŏng Hwan'guk. "16 segi mal 17 segi ch'o sasangsa ŭi hŭrŭm sok esŏ pon *Unyŏng-jŏn*" [*Unyŏng-jŏn* in the intellectual current of the late sixteenth and early seventeenth centuries]. In *Han'guk kojŏn yŏsŏng munhak yŏn'gu* [Korean classical women's literature research], ed. Han'guk kŏjon yŏsŏng munhak-hoe, 7:261–292. Seoul: Wŏrin, 2003.

Chŏng Kyubok. "*Unyŏng-jŏn* ŭi munje" [Questions about *Unyŏng-jŏn*]. *Kodae munhwa* 11 (May 1970): 115–124.

Chŏng Nakch'an, Yi Tonggi, and Ch'ae Hwigyun, eds. *Han'guk ŭi chŏnt'ong kyuyuk* [Traditional education in Korea]. Kyŏngsan: Yŏngnam taehakkyo ch'ulp'anbu, 2002.

Chŏng Pyŏn'guk. *Han'guk kojŏn siga-ron* [Poetic theory of classical Korean poem-songs]. Seoul: Sin'gu munhwasa, 2000.

Choung, Haechang, and Han Hyong-jo. *Confucian Philosophy in Korea.* Sŏngnam: Academy of Korean Studies, 1996.

Clark, Cyril Drummond Le Gros. *The Prose-Poetry of Su Tung-P'o.* New York: Paragon Book Reprint, 1964.

Deuchler, Martina. *The Confucian Transformation of Korea: A Study of Society and Ideology.* Cambridge: Harvard University Press, 1992.

_____. "Propagating Female Virtues in Chosŏn Korea." In *Women and Confucian Cultures in Premodern China, Korea, and Japan,* ed. Dorothy Ko, JaHyun Kim Haboush, and Joan R. Piggott, 142–169. Berkeley: University of California Press, 2003.

Duncan, John. "The *Naehun* and the Politics of Gender in Fifteenth-Century Korea." In *Creative Women of Korea: The Fifteenth through the Twentieth Centuries,* ed. Young-Key Kim-Renaud, 26–57. Armonk, N.Y.: M. E. Sharpe, 2004.

_____. *The Origins of the Chosŏn Dynasty.* Seattle: University of Washington Press, 2000.

Eckert, Carter J., et al. *Korea Old and New, A History.* Seoul: Ilchokak, 1990.

Egan, Ronald C. *Word, Image, and Deed in the Life of Su Shi.* Cambridge: Harvard University Press, 1994.

Fang, Chaoying. *The Asami Library: A Descriptive Catalogue.* Ed. Elizabeth Huff. Berkeley: University of California Press, 1969.

Han'guk kojŏn yŏsŏng munhak-hoe, ed. *Kojŏn munhak kwa yŏsŏng hwaja: kŭ kŭl ssŭgi ŭi chŏllyak* [Classical literature and women's voices: Their writing and strategies]. Seoul: Wŏrin, 2003.

Han'guk minjok munhwa taebaekkwa sajŏn [Encyclopedia of Korean culture]. 28 vols. Sŏngnam: Han'guk chŏngsin munhwa yŏn'guwŏn, 1994.

Han'guk minsok taesajŏn [Encyclopedia of Korean folk culture]. 2 vols. Seoul: Minjok munhwasa, 1991.

Harvey, Youngsook Kim. *Six Korean Women: The Socialization of Shamans.* St. Paul, Minn.: West Publishing, 1979.

Hŏ Mija. *Han'guk yŏryu munhak ron, kojŏnp'yŏn* [Literary theory of Korean women writers, classical works]. Seoul: Sŏngsin yŏja taehakkyo ch'ulp'anbu, 1991.

_____. *Han'guk yŏsŏng munhak yŏn'gu* [A study of literature by Korean women]. Seoul: T'aehaksa, 1996.

Hoyt, James. *Soaring Phoenixes and Prancing Dragons: A Historical Survey of Korean Classical Literature.* Seoul: Jimoondang, 2000.

Huang, Martin W. *Desire and Fictional Narrative in Late Imperial China.* Cambridge: Harvard University Asia Center, 2001.

Hwang Chaegun, Kim Kyŏngnam, and Mun Pokhŭi. *Han'guk munhak kwa yŏsŏng* [Korean literature and women]. Seoul: Pakijŏng, 1997.

Hwang P'aegang. *Chosŏn wangjo sosŏl yŏn'gu* [A study of novels of the Chosŏn dynasty]. Seoul: Tan'guk taehakkyo ch'ulp'anbu, 1999.

Ihwa Chungguk yŏsŏng munhak yŏn'gu-hoe, ed. *Tong asia yŏsŏng ŭi kiwŏn:* Yŏllyŏ-jŏn'*-e taehan yŏsŏnghakchŏk t'amgu* [The origins of East Asian women: A woman's study investigation concerning the *Yollyŏ-jŏn*]. Seoul: Ihwa yŏja taehakkyo ch'ulp'anbu, 2002.

Ihwa ŏmun hakhoe, ed. *Uri munhak ŭi yŏsŏngsŏng, namsŏngsŏng: kojŏn munhak p'yŏn* [Female and male temperaments in our (i.e., Korean) literature: Classical literature edition]. Seoul: Wŏrin, 2001.

Ihwa yŏja taehakkyo, Han'guk yŏsŏng yŏn'guso, ed. *Han'guk yŏsŏng kwan'gye charyo chip, kŭnsep'yŏn (pŏpchŏn)* [Collected materials related to Korean women, modern history edition (legal codes)]. 2 vols. Seoul: Ihwa yŏja taehakkyo ch'ulp'anbu, 1989.

———. *Han'guk yŏsŏngsa charyo chip, Chosŏn wangjo sillok* [Collected materials on Korean women's history, Veritable records of the Chosŏn dynasty]. 11 vols. Seoul: Ihwa yŏja taehakkyo ch'ulp'anbu, 1992–1998.

Jackson, Rosemary. *Fantasy: The Literature of Subversion.* London: Methuen, 1981.

Jeon, Sang-woon. *A History of Science in Korea.* Seoul: Jimoondang, 1998.

Kim Haboush, JaHyun. "Dead Bodies in the Postwar Discourse of Identity in Seventeenth-Century Korea: Subversion and Literary Production in the Private Sector." *Journal of Asian Studies* 62 (May 2003): 415–442.

———. *The Memoirs of Lady Hyegyŏng: The Autobiographical Writings of a Crown Princess of Eighteenth-Century Korea.* Berkeley: University of California Press, 1996.

———. "Versions and Subversions: Patriarchy and Polygamy in Korean Narratives." In *Women and Confucian Cultures in Premodern China, Korea, and Japan,* ed. Dorothy Ko, JaHyun Kim Haboush, and Joan R. Piggott, 279–303. Berkeley: University of California Press, 2003.

Kim, Hŭnggyu. "Chosŏn Fiction in Chinese." In *A History of Korean Literature,* ed. Peter H. Lee, 261–272. Cambridge: Cambridge University Press, 2003.

Kim Hyŏnyŏng et al. *Chosŏn sidae sahoe ŭi mosŭp* [Social features of the Chosŏn period]. Seoul: Chimmundang, 2003.

Kim, Kichung. "Unheard Voices: The Life of the *Nobi* in O Hwimun's *Swaemirok.*" *Korean Studies* 27 (2003): 108–137.

Kim Kyŏngmi. "*Unyŏng-jŏn*-e nat'anan yŏsŏng sŏsulja ŭi ŭiŭi" [The significance of the female narrator in *Unyŏng-jŏn*]. In *Han'guk kŏjon yŏsŏng munhak yŏn'gu* [Korean classical women's literature research], ed. Han'guk kŏjon yŏsŏng munhak-hoe, 4:35–65. Seoul: Wŏrin, 2002.

Kim Myŏnghŭi et al. *Chosŏn sidae yŏsŏng munhak kwa sasang* [Women's literature and thought in the Chosŏn period]. Seoul: Ihŏe, 2003.

Kim Yŏju. *Chosŏn hugi yŏsŏng munhak ŭi chaejomyŏng* [Reilluminating the women's literature of the late Chosŏn period]. Seoul: Sŏngsin yŏja taehakkyo ch'ulp'anbu, 2004.

Kim Yongsuk. *Chosŏnjo kungjung p'ungsok yŏn'gu* [A study of the palace customs in the Chosŏn dynasty]. Seoul: Iljisa, 1987.

______. *Han'guk yŏsok sa* [A history of Korean women's customs]. Seoul: Minŭmsa, 1989.

Kim Yŏnsuk. *Kososŏl ŭi yŏsŏng chuŭijŏk yŏn'gu* [A study of feminism in classical novels]. Seoul: Kukhak charyowŏn, 2002.

Ko, Dorothy; JaHyun Kim Haboush; and Joan R. Piggott, eds. *Women and Confucian Cultures in Premodern China, Korea, and Japan.* Berkeley: University of California Press, 2003.

Kwak Chŏngsik et al. *Han'guk munhak sasangsa* [An ideological history of Korean literature]. Seoul: Sinji sŏwŏn, 1998.

Lee, Ki-baik. *A New History of Korea.* Trans. Edward W. Wagner with Edward J. Shultz. Cambridge: Harvard University Press, 1984.

Legge, James. *The Chinese Classics.* Vol. 4: *The She King.* Hong Kong: Hong Kong University Press, 1960.

Liu, Wu-Chi. *An Introduction to Chinese Literature.* Bloomington: Indiana University Press, 1966.

Millet, Kate. *Sexual Politics.* London: Abacus, 1972.

Min Yŏngdae. *Chosŏn sidae kungjung sŏsol yŏn'gu* [A study of Chosŏn-period palace novels]. Seoul: Yŏngnak, 2004.

Morris, Pam. *Literature and Feminism.* Oxford: Blackwell, 1993.

O Chonggŭn and Paek Miae. *Chosŏnjo kajŏng sosŏl yŏn'gu* [A study of family novels of the Chosŏn dynasty]. Seoul: Wŏrin, 2001.

Pak Chu. *Chosŏn sidae ŭi chŏngp'yo chŏngch'aek* [Policies concerning expressions of virtue in the Chosŏn period]. Seoul: Ilchogak, 1997.

Pak Hyŏnsuk. *Chosŏn kŏn'gukki ŭi munhak-ron* [Literary ideology in the age of the foundation of Chosŏn]. Seoul: Ihoe munhwasa, 2002.

Pak Kijung. *Chosŏnjo ŭi kayo* [Songs of the Chosŏn dynasty]. Seoul: Sŏngmun'gak, 1989.

Pak Kisŏk. "*Unyŏng-jŏn*" [The tale of Unyŏng]. In *Han'guk kojŏn sosŏl chakp'um non* [Treatise on classical Korean novels], 713. Quoted in Cho Hŭiung, *Kojŏn sosŏl ibon mongnok* [Catalogue of alternative titles for classical novels]. Seoul: Chimmundang, 1999.

Pak T'aesang. *Chosŏnjo aejŏng sosŏl yŏn'gu* [A study of romance novels of the Chosŏn period]. Seoul: T'aehaksa, 1999.

Pettid, Michael J. "Devoted Wives and Chaste Maidens: Didactic Literature and Virtuous Women in Chosŏn Korea." In *Korea: Language, Knowledge and Society*, ed. Gi-Hyun Shin, 85–95. Canberra: Australian National University, 2003.

______. "From Abandoned Daughter to Shaman Matriarch: An Analysis of the *Pari Kongju Muga*, a Korean Shamanistic Song." Ph.D. diss., University of Hawaii at Manoa, 1999.

______. "Late-Chosŏn Society as Reflected in a Shamanistic Narrative: An Analysis of the *Pari kongju muga*." *Korean Studies* 24 (2000): 113–141.

Pihl, Marshall R. *The Korean Singer of Tales*. Cambridge: Harvard University Asia Center, 1994.

Pu Kilman. *Chosŏn sidae panggak-bon ch'ulp'an yŏn'gu* [A study of the publication of *panggak-bon* in the Chosŏn period]. Seoul: Sŏul ch'ulp'an midiŏ, 2003.

Ryan, Michael. *Literary Theory: A Practical Introduction*. Oxford: Blackwell, 1999.

Shigeyoshi, Obata. *The Works of Li Po, the Chinese Poet*. New York: Paragon Book Reprint, 1964.

Shultz, Edward J. *Generals and Scholars: Military Rule in Medieval Korea*. Honolulu: University of Hawai'i Press, 2000.

Sin Myŏngho. *Kunggwŏl ŭi kkot: kungnyŏ* [Flowers of the palace: Palace women]. Seoul: Sigongsa, 2004.

Sin Ŭn'gyŏng. *Kojŏn si tasi ilgi* [Rereading classical poetry]. Seoul: Pogosa, 1997.

So Chaeyong. "*Unyŏng-jŏn* yŏn'gu" [A study of *Unyŏng-jŏn*]. *Asea yŏn'gu* 14 (March 1971): 153–179.

Wawrytko, Sandra A. "Prudence and Prurience: Historical Roots of the Confucian Conundrum Concerning Women, Sexuality, and Power." In *The Sage and the Second Sex: Confucianism, Ethics, and Gender,* ed. Chenyang Li, 163–197. Chicago: Open Court, 2000.

Yi Hyesun et al. *Han'guk kojŏn yŏsŏng chakka yŏn'gu* [A study of classical Korean women writers]. Seoul: T'aehaksa, 2000.

———. *Uri hanmunhaksa ŭi yŏsŏng ŭi insik* [Understandings of women in Korean literary history]. Seoul: Chimmundang, 2003.

Yi Man'gyu. *Chosŏn kyoyuksa* [History of education in Korea]. 2 vols. Seoul: K'raun p'an, 1986.

Yi Sanggu. *17 segi aejŏng chŏn'gi sosŏl* [Seventeenth-century tales of wonder romance novels]. Seoul: Wŏrin, 1999.

Yi Sun'gu. "Chosŏn sidae ŭi sŏngnihak kwa yŏsŏng" [Women and Song Confucianism in the Chosŏn period]. In *Uri yŏsŏng ŭi yŏksa* [The history of Korean women], ed. Han'guk yŏsŏng yŏn'guso, 163–189. Seoul: Ch'ŏngnyŏnsa, 1999.

Yi Wŏnho. *Chosŏn sidae kyoyuk ŭi yŏn'gu* [A study of education during the Chosŏn period]. Seoul: Munŭmsa, 2002.

Yi Yunsŏk, Otani Morishige, and Chŏng Myŏnggi, eds. *Sech'aek kososŏl yŏn'gu* [A study of book-lending of classical novels]. Seoul: Hyean, 2003.

Yu Tongsik. *Han'guk mugyo ŭi yŏksa wa kujo* [The history and structure of Korean shamanism]. Seoul: Yŏnse taehakkyo, 1978.

Index

INSTITUTE OF EAST ASIAN STUDIES PUBLICATIONS SERIES

CHINA RESEARCH MONOGRAPHS (CRM)

40. Frederic Wakeman, Jr., and Wen-hsin Yeh, eds. *Shanghai Sojourners*, 1992
42. Barry C. Keenan. *Imperial China's Last Classical Academies: Social Change in the Lower Yangzi, 1864–1911*, 1994
43. Ole Bruun. *Business and Bureaucracy in a Chinese City: An Ethnography of Private Business Households in Contemporary China*, 1993
44. Wei Li. *The Chinese Staff System: A Mechanism for Bureaucratic Control and Integration*, 1994
45. Ye Wa and Joseph W. Esherick. *Chinese Archives: An Introductory Guide*, 1996
46. Melissa Brown, ed. *Negotiating Ethnicities in China and Taiwan*, 1996
47. David Zweig and Chen Changgui. *China's Brain Drain to the United States: Views of Overseas Chinese Students and Scholars in the 1990s*, 1995
48. Elizabeth J. Perry, ed. *Putting Class in Its Place: Worker Identities in East Asia*, 1996
49. Wen-hsin Yeh, ed. *Landscape, Culture, and Power in Chinese Society*, 1998
50. Gail Hershatter, Emily Honig, Susan Mann, and Lisa Rofel, comps. and eds. *Guide to Women's Studies in China*, 1999
51. Wen-hsin Yeh, ed. *Modern Chinese Literary and Cultural Studies: Theoretical Issues*, 2000
52. Marilyn A. Levine and Chen San-ching, eds. *The Guomindang in Europe: A Sourcebook of Documents*, 2000
53. David N. Keightley. *The Ancestral Landscape: Time, Space, and Community in Late Shang China*, 2000
54. Peter M. Worthing. *Occupation and Revolution: China and the Vietnamese August Revolution of 1945*, 2001.
55. Guo Qitao. *Exorcism and Money: The Symbolic World of the Five-Fury Spirits in Late Imperial China*, 2003
56. Robert J. Antony. *Like Froth Floating on the Sea: The World of Pirates and Seafarers in Late Imperial South China*, 2003
57. Joshua A. Fogel, ed. *The Role of Japan in Liang Qichao's Introduction of Modern Western Civilization to China*, 2004
58. Xin Liu, ed. *New Reflections on Anthropological Studies of (greater) China*, 2004
59. Virginia Harper Ho. *Labor Dispute Resolution in China*, 2003.
60. Jon Eugene von Kowallis. *The Subtle Revolution: Poets of the "Old Schools" during Late Qing and Early Republican China*, 2006
61. Joseph W. Esherick, Wen-hsin Yeh, and Madeleine Zelin, eds. *Empire, Nation, and Beyond: Chinese History in Late Imperial and Modern Times—a Festschrift in Honor of Frederic Wakeman*, 2006
62. David Strand, Sherman Cochran, and Wen-hsin Yeh, eds. *Cities in Motion: Interior, Coast, and Diaspora in Transnational China*, 2007

KOREA RESEARCH MONOGRAPHS (KRM)

13. Vipan Chandra. *Imperialism, Resistance, and Reform in Late Nineteenth-Century Korea: Enlightenment and the Independence Club*, 1988
14. Seok Choong Song. *Explorations in Korean Syntax and Semantics*, 1988
15. Robert A. Scalapino and Dalchoong Kim, eds. *Asian Communism: Continuity and Transition*, 1988
16. Chong-Sik Lee and Se-Hee Yoo, eds. *North Korea in Transition*, 1991
17. Nicholas Eberstadt and Judith Banister. *The Population of North Korea*, 1992
18. Hong Yung Lee and Chung Chongwook, eds. *Korean Options in a Changing International Order*, 1993
19. Tae Hwan Ok and Hong Yung Lee, eds. *Prospects for Change in North Korea*, 1994
20. Chai-sik Chung. *A Korean Confucian Encounter with the Modern World: Yi Hang-no and the West*, 1995
21. Myung Hun Kang. *The Korean Business Conglomerate: Chaebol Then and Now*, 1996
25. Jeong-Hyun Shin. *The Trap of History: Understanding Korean Short Stories*, 1998
26. Hyung Il Pai and Timothy R. Tangherlini, eds. *Nationalism and the Construction of Korean Identity*, 1999
27. Nathan Hesselink, ed. *Contemporary Directions: Korean Folk Music Engaging the Twentieth Century and Beyond*, 2002

28. Choi Byonghyon, trans. *The Book of Corrections: Reflections on the National Crisis during the Japanese Invasion of Korea, 1592–1598* (by Yu Songnyong), 2002
29. Margaret Walker Dilling. *Stories inside Stories: Music in the Making of the Korean Olympic Ceremonies*, 2007
30. Hyuk-Rae Kim and Bok Song, eds. *Modern Korean Society: Its Development and Prospect*, 2007
31. Hun Joo Park. *Diseased* Dirigisme: *The Political Sources of Financial Policy toward Small Business in Korea*, 2008
32. Michael Finch. *Min Yŏnghwan: The Selected Writings of a Late Chosŏn Diplomat*, 2008
33. Michael J. Pettid. Unyŏng-jōn: *A Love Affair at the Royal Palace of Chosŏn Korea*. Trans. Kil Cha and Michael J. Pettid. Intro. and annot. Michael J. Pettid.

JAPAN RESEARCH MONOGRAPHS (JRM)

10. Steve Rabson, trans. *Okinawa: Two Postwar Novellas* by Ōshiro Tatsuhiro and Higashi Mineo. Introduction and afterword by Steve Rabson. 1996 (2d printing, corrected and updated [1998])
12. James W. White. *The Demography of Sociopolitical Conflict in Japan, 1721–1846*, 1992
13. Winston Davis. *The Moral and Political Naturalism of Baron Katō Hiroyuki*, 1996
14. Michael H. Gibbs. *Struggle and Purpose in Postwar Japanese Unionism*, 2000
15. Ronan Alves Pereira and Hideaki Matsuoka, eds. *Japanese Religions in and beyond the Japanese Diaspora*, 2007

RESEARCH PAPERS AND POLICY STUDIES (RPPS)

24. Joyce K. Kallgren, Noordin Sopiee, and Soedjati Djiwandono, eds. *ASEAN and China: An Evolving Relationship*, 1988
29. Richard Holton and Wang Xi, eds. *U.S.-China Economic Relations: Present and Future*, 1989
30. Sadako Ogata. *Normalization with China: A Comparative Study of U.S. and Japanese Processes*, 1989
32. Leo E. Rose and Kamal Matinuddin, eds. *Beyond Afghanistan: The Emerging U.S.-Pakistan Relations*, 1990
33. Clark Neher and Wiwat Mungkandi, eds. *U.S.-Thailand Relations in a New International Era*, 1990
34. Robert Sutter and Han Sungjoo, eds. *Korea-U.S. Relations in a Changing World*, 1990
35. Harry H. Kendall and Clara Joewono, eds. *Japan, ASEAN, and the United States*, 1990
36. Robert A. Scalapino and Gennady I. Chufrin, eds. *Asia in the 1990s: American and Soviet Perspectives*, 1990
37. Chong-Sik Lee, ed. *In Search of a New Order in East Asia*, 1991
38. Leo E. Rose and Eric Gonsalves, eds. *Toward a New World Order: Adjusting U.S.-India Relations*, 1992
40. Yufan Hao. *Dilemma and Decision: An Organizational Perspective on American China Policy Making*, 1997
41. Frederic Wakeman Jr. and Wang Xi, eds. *China's Quest for Modernization: A Historical Perspective*, 1997
42. Loraine A. West and Yaohui Zhao, eds. *Rural Labor Flows in China*, 2000
43. Shalendra D. Sharma, ed. *The Asia-Pacific in the New Millennium: Geopolitics, Security, and Foreign Policy*, 2000
44. David Arase, ed. *The Challenge of Change: East Asia in the New Millennium*, 2003

SPECIAL PUBLICATIONS

Sp. Kaidi Zhan. *The Strategies of Politeness in the Chinese Language*, 1992

Sp. Theodore Han and John Li. *Tiananmen Square Spring 1989: A Chronology of the Chinese Democracy Movement*, 1992

Sp. Phyllis L. Thompson, ed. *Dear Alice: Letters Home from American Teachers Learning to Live in China*, 1998

Sp. Samuel Hawley. *The Imjin War: Japan's Sixteenth-Century Invasion of Korea and Attempt to Conquer China*, 2005

Sp. Robert A. Scalapino. *From Leavenworth to Lhasa: Living in a Revolutionary Era*, 2008

These are new and selected publications. Write for a complete list and prices.

E-mail: easia@uclink.berkeley.edu

http://ieas.berkeley.edu/publications

INTERNATIONAL AND AREA STUDIES

John Lie, Dean

International and Area Studies at the University of California, Berkeley, comprises four groups: international and comparative studies, area studies, teaching programs, and services to international programs.

INSTITUTE OF EAST ASIAN STUDIES
UNIVERSITY OF CALIFORNIA, BERKELEY

The Institute of East Asian Studies, now a part of Berkeley International and Area Studies, was established at the University of California at Berkeley in the fall of 1978 to promote research and teaching on the cultures and societies of China, Japan, and Korea. It amalgamates the following research and instructional centers and programs: the Center for Buddhist Studies, the Center for Chinese Studies, the Center for Japanese Studies, the Center for Korean Studies, the Group in Asian Studies, the East Asia National Resource Center, and the Inter-university Program for Chinese Language Studies.

www.ingramcontent.com/pod-product-compliance
Lightning Source LLC
LaVergne TN
LVHW041929090826
845145LV00017B/2786

* 9 7 8 1 5 5 7 2 9 0 9 3 9 *